Quiet London

quiet corners

Quiet London

quiet corners

Siobhan Wall

F

FRANCES LINCOLN LIMITED
PUBLISHERS

Frances Lincoln Limited
74–77 White Lion Street
London N1 9PF

Quiet London: Quiet Corners
Copyright © 2014 Frances Lincoln Limited
Text and photographs copyright © 2014 Siobhan Wall

Except photographs copyright © page 30 Rosmond Milner; page 52
Bamford Haybarn at The Berkeley; page 64 Nicki Davis; page 126
Number Sixteen

First Frances Lincoln edition 2014

A catalogue record for this book is available from the British Library

ISBN 978-0-7112-3560-1

Edited and designed by Jane Havell Associates
Printed and bound in China
9 8 7 6 5 4 3 2 1

FRONT COVER Kensington Roof Gardens; BACK COVER Jamyang
Buddhist Centre; page 1 St Olave's Church; page 2 Holland Park;
page 6 Langton Chapel, St Mary's Church, Barnes; page 9 Keats
Grove, Hampstead

Contents

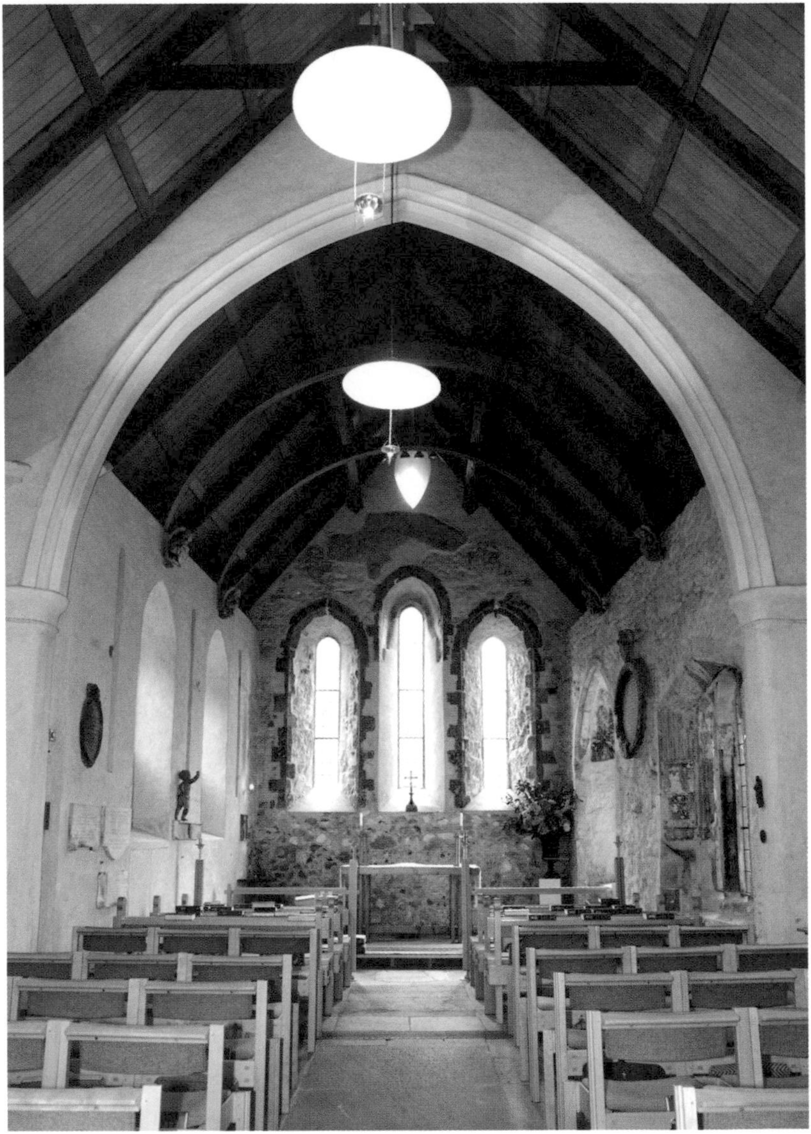

Introduction

I first started doing research around six years ago on tranquil places for *Quiet London*, the first illustrated guide to places to eat, drink, read, wander and browse in the capital. From the moment it was published, this small book was appreciated by many readers. It seemed that a few people not only bought the guide for themselves, but also for close friends as a way of saying, 'I am giving you some quiet time – implicit permission to find tranquil moments in your life.' This was very encouraging, as was the fact that when I contacted the meditation centres, bookshops, cafés and libraries to ask if they wanted to be included in the new *Quiet London* books, people welcomed me with open arms. This was a wonderful opportunity to meet my readers and we talked enthusiastically about our favourite quiet places.

Starting to do research for three new *Quiet London* books on Culture, Quiet Corners and Food & Drink, I realised that discovering calm, peaceful places was not just about avoiding city noise and anonymous crowds but about finding beautiful, serene locations which would also make people feel happy. I only shot photographs in the daytime, but I wanted to come back for the 'Midnight Apothecary' in the pretty Brunel Museum garden, to drink blackberry Martinis surrounded by tall sunflowers after dark. As someone who loves the excitement of visiting exhibitions and going to concerts, I also knew that there were times when I needed to seek out a small garden or a quiet library just for the pleasure of being alone with my thoughts.

Just before setting up my tripod, I could sit in ancient chapels, listening to the closest thing to silence, surrounded by dark wooden pews and the carved effigies of people who were alive when the church was newly built. St Margaret Lothbury at dusk was an especially calm place, where it seemed time was suspended inside these ancient walls, with only pale candle flames to soften the slowly fading light. Not advertised on billboards, not part of a 'special offer', not clamouring for attention on social media, such rare moments of unhurried, gradual wonder are open not only to me, but to anyone who enters this hallowed building.

I was delighted to have the opportunity to discover and write about even more quiet places in London, not only because there were many I couldn't include in the first book, but also because some new places opened, which suggested to me that even though London is getting increasingly crowded, more people appreciate tranquil places than ever before. Music-free places that didn't exist a few years ago are the friendly Suzzle in Brick Lane and the Dalston Curve Garden Café. This informal Hackney tea room was created on the old Eastern Curve railway which used to link Dalston Junction Station to the goods yard and the North London Line. The Dalston Curve Garden, in particular, demonstrates the precious enthusiasm and commitment of local people, who put considerable effort into creating intimate green spaces in densely packed urban areas. It is heartening to see such places blossom and thrive, especially in neighbourhoods where new developments could easily crowd out community initiatives. It was also deeply satisfying to find that many other people shared my enthusiasm for quiet places, whether by weeding King Henry's Walk community garden or tending the vegetable plots behind Rosebery Lodge in Dulwich Park.

Recent research suggests that people's mental health can be considerably improved if they walk among trees. Children also develop better cognitive function and emotional maturity if they can play in parks and woodland, partly because these are imaginative spaces to run around and enact stories in – healthy ways to integrate growing limbs with developing brains. So this book is not just for sedentary adults, who find it hard to entice each other away from digital screens. It is also for children, who need to discover the pleasure of running among undergrowth, dipping sticks in ponds and unexpectedly catching sight of a roe deer in a clearing. In his book *Feral: Searching for Enchantment on the Frontiers of Rewilding*, George Monbiot wrote about his longing to see primary schools take their pupils 'for one afternoon a week, to run wild in the woods'. He claimed that there isn't enough woodland in urban areas to make this happen, but I think in London there may be more wild spaces than he imagines. Familiar large parks have been transformed over the past five years, and are no longer flat expanses of lawn with shrubbery around their sparse edges. Walthamstow's Lloyd Park has free 'nature explorers' activities for the under-5s with themes including hungry caterpillars. Older children can join in their evening bat walks, and there is outdoor tai chi for people over 50, suggesting that there are many different ways for people of all ages to encounter nature and find relaxation in big cities.

The three new *Quiet London* books also celebrate the existence of places that have barely changed for centuries, such as Mitcham Common with its wide open grassland and Epping Forest with its ancient pollarded trees, muntjac deer and nuthatches. With more than

8 million people living in Greater London (according to the 2011 census), and a few million more travelling into the city to work each day, it would seem impossible to find some quiet respite and time away from the demands of others. In 1981, when I first arrived in London, there were around 2 million fewer people living here; in six years' time, it is expected that the numbers will rise to 9 million. At first glance there seem to be few hidden, private corners in this sprawling, unrelentingly busy city. However, with an unremitting desire to seek out tranquil places wherever they may be, I opened doors that might otherwise have remained closed and quietly followed well-worn, but less well-known, footpaths. I was inspired by what I saw. One afternoon I came across Octavia's Orchard: mini portable gardens placed around the South Bank complex for a few weeks in the summer of 2013. Inspired by the ideas of the nineteenth-century reformer Octavia Hill, these diminutive meadows were intended to highlight the lack of access to green spaces in built-up areas. On one of the containers was written a question by Octavia Hill: 'Does it not seem that the quiet influence of nature is more restful to Londoners than anything else?' This inspiring woman called London parks and gardens 'outdoor sitting rooms', where anyone could sit or wander.

I want to return to many places and slowly appreciate their calm delights. I was entranced by Peckham Rye Community Wildlife Garden, with its insect hotel. This secluded nature reserve is typical of the carefully tended green spaces which encourage biodiversity for living creatures, and peaceful oases for busy humans. No longer neglected, London parks are experiencing a heyday and I am delighted that I can let people know about their more secret corners. And if there was one quiet, but exciting, thing I would still like to do when I am next in South London? It is to go for a guided walk in Deptford Creek, following the route of the Ravensbourne River by wading through thick, grey mud up to my knees.

Parks, gardens & open spaces

Horniman Museum Gardens

100 London Road, Forest Hill SE23 3PQ ☎ 020 8699 1872
Free www.horniman.ac.uk
Open Monday–Saturday 7.15am–sunset, Sundays and Bank Holidays 8am–sunset, closed Christmas Day. Nature Trail 9am–4pm, but may be closed at short notice in bad weather
Train Forest Hill **Bus** 176, 185, 197, 365, P4
The gardens are wheelchair accessible but the lawns have a steep gradient. Limited on-site car parking is available for disabled visitors, call for details

The gardens surrounding the magnificent Arts & Crafts Horniman Museum are inviting and varied. From the vegetable plots with their educational information sheets to the sweeping lawns behind, this is a wonderful place to wander and amble south of the river. Frederick John Horniman was a wealthy nineteenth-century tea trader who wanted to show his collection of artefacts to Londoners; the planted beds reflect his botanical interests, bringing a diversity of plants from all over the world to a magnificent London hillside. As well as a Dutch barn and carved totem pole, look out for the unusual sundials placed around the gardens.

Lloyd Park

Forest Road, Walthamstow E17 4PP, other entrances in Winns Terrace, Winns Avenue, Brettenham Road, Aveling Park Road
Free www.walthamforest.gov.uk/pages/servicechild/lloyd-park.aspx, www.friendsoflloydpark.org.uk
Open Monday–Saturday 7.30am–dusk, Sunday 9am–dusk
Tube Blackhorse Road, Walthamstow Central **Bus** 34, 97, 123, 215, 275, 357
The park is wheelchair accessible

The family of William Morris moved into Water House, as the gallery used to be known, in 1848 when the artist and writer was just 14. He used to play here long before it became a public park in 1900, and it is easy to see how he was inspired by the medieval moat and wild flowers surrounding his parents' home. Recently refurbished, it now has a William Morris garden, planted with many of the flowers found in his textile and wallpaper designs. With its formal terraced gardens, new wetland area and neat lawns, the variety in this East London park is what makes it special. And if the weather is poor, you can always visit an exhibition in the modern Winns Gallery inside the Aveling Centre.

Morden Park

Morden Hall Road, SM4 5JD ☎ 020 8545 3667
Free www.merton.gov.uk/environment/openspaces/parks/parks_in_the_morden_
area/mordenpark.htm
Open Monday–Friday 8am–dusk, Saturday, Sunday and Bank Holidays 9am–dusk
Tube Morden **Train** Morden South **Bus** 80, 93, 154, 293
The paths are wheelchair accessible

This well-loved park is a tranquil place to walk and observe the landscape change
through the seasons. The ancient trees are its main attraction, from Turkey oaks,
grey poplars and limes to chestnuts; they are magnificent in summer and strikingly
beautiful when bare in winter. New trees such as holly, blackthorn, yew, silver birch
and rowan have all been recently planted by volunteers and schoolchildren, increasing
diversity in the park as well as teaching younger nature lovers about native species. In
the south-eastern corner there is a wetland area, where wildlife congregates around
the Pyl Brook, an important habitat for both visible creatures such as frogs and newts,
and more shy animals that depend on being out of sight and left alone.

Grosvenor Square Garden
Grosvenor Square, W1K 4AF **Free**
Open Daily 8am–dusk
Tube Bond Street, Marble Arch
Bus 2, 6, 7, 10, 16, 23, 36, 73, 94, 98, 159, 189, 436
Grosvenor Square is wheelchair accessible

Stone paths cut across this grand Mayfair square full of tall plane trees near the American Embassy. There are a few wooden benches to sit and admire the Franklin Roosevelt Memorial, erected in 1948 soon after he died. At the eastern edge of the park there's a small garden and oak pergola, a permanent memorial to the British victims of the World Trade Center and Pentagon attacks on 11 September 2001. This quiet arbour is an unexpectedly intimate space for reflection in the middle of an area surrounded by rather anonymous, stone-clad buildings. With its white Bianca roses, Grecian-inspired portico and simple columns, this is a beautiful place to sit and ponder.

Princes Square

Imperial College, South Kensington SW7 2AZ
Free www.imperial.ac.uk
Open All day every day
Tube South Kensington **Bus** 9, 10, 52, 70, 74, 360, 452
Princes Square is wheelchair accessible

One of the world's best science-based universities, Imperial College London not only excels in teaching and research, it is also located in one of the most beautiful areas of London, close to Hyde Park and the resplendent Albert Memorial. There are two lawns surrounded by college buildings – Princes Lawn to the east side of Exhibition Road, and Queen's Lawn to the west. After a visit to the often-crowded Victoria & Albert and Science Museums, these verdant squares are a good place to sit and listen to the wind in the trees.

Cannizaro Park

West Side Common, Wimbledon SW19 4UE
Free www.cannizaropark.com
Open Monday–Friday 8am–dusk, Saturday, Sunday and Bank Holidays 9am–dusk
Tube Wimbledon **Bus** 93, 200, 493
Most of the park is wheelchair accessible

Cannizaro Park is a gorgeous, 35-acre, Grade II-listed park not far from Wimbledon Village. It has almost everything – a pond with wildfowl, a grand country house with a terrace café, a sunken garden full of brightly coloured flowers, and rolling lawns dotted with magnificent cedars of Lebanon. As well as offering sweeping vistas and woodland walks, it has secluded spots, including a herb garden where you can sit on a sheltered wooden bench near a bronze statue of a small dog. There are many places to wander, with paths leading down to formal terraces. Near the entrance, catch a glimpse of the small aviary filled with brightly coloured birds.

World Peace Garden

6 South Hill Park, Hampstead NW3 2SB ☎ 07956 191567
Free www.worldpeacegardencamden.org
Open Daily 10am–6pm, subject to weather conditions (it can be slippery after rain)
Tube Hampstead, Belsize Park **Train** Hampstead Heath
Bus 24, 46, 168, 268, C11
This steep garden is not wheelchair accessible. Guide dogs only, and children must be accompanied by an adult

This sanctuary garden alongside the railway track was designed to encourage inner peace and reflection. An impressive labour of love, it took over eight years to create. One nice feature is the display of glass tiles near the entrance by artist Melissa Fairbanks. In spring, wisteria climbs up the tall trees, and children are encouraged to write messages about how they would like the world to be when they grow up. Look out for the cherry tree planted by Eva Schloss, stepsister of Anne Frank, and the seat that encourages 'letting go' of our worries and everyday concerns.

Peckham Rye Park and Common

Peckham Rye, Homestall Road, Colyton Road and Strakers Road, SE15
☎ 07974 325 906 **Free** www.foprp.org.uk
Open Daily 7.30am–dusk in winter, 7.30–9pm to August,
Community Wildlife Garden 10am–3.30pm in winter, 10am–5pm in summer
Train Nunhead, East Dulwich, Peckham Rye, Honor Oak Park
Bus 12, 37, 40, 63, 78, 112, 176, 185, 197, 312, 343, 363, 484, P4, P12, P13,
The park and common are both wheelchair accessible

Peckham Rye Park and Common were restored a few years ago and are now very enticing places to wander at any time of year. Walk through ornamental gardens, past flowing streams, and lose yourself in broadleaf woodland, maybe ending up beside the tranquil lake. This is one of the few London parks with an arboretum, so bring an alfresco lunch to share among the trees in the scenic picnic area. The Sexby Gardens are particularly beautiful, with roses climbing over simple pergolas and winding paths that encourage afternoon rambling. If the Community Wildlife Garden is open – a secluded enclave within the park – the volunteers can tell you about the specially designed tall insect homes and what they are growing in their vegetable plots.

London Fields

London Fields Westside, E8 3EU, entrances also on Lansdowne Drive,
Richmond Road and Martello Street
☎ Hackney Parks Service 020 8356 8428/9
Free www.hackney.gov.uk/cp-londonfields
Open All day every day
Train London Fields **Bus** 26, 48, 55, 106, 236, 254, 388, 394
The park is wheelchair accessible

Despite being one of London's busiest parks, the open grassland surrounded by
plane trees feels surprisingly relaxed. You can't miss the stunning wildflower meadow
planted with poppies, pink cosmos and other perennials and annuals. Instead of
neatly mown but rather dull grass, the centre of the park now has a visually stunning
focal point, much appreciated by bees, butterflies and other insects. London Fields is
still described as common land because it was historically used for grazing animals
as well as being on a route for moving animals to Smithfield Market. This is an ideal
place to stroll on summer evenings after work, when the low sun turns the meadow
into a romantic, floral backdrop for Londoners from all backgrounds.

Victoria Park

Grove Road, E9 7DE, entrances also on Gore Road, Park Road
☎ Park Ranger 020 8985 5699, Tower Hamlets Parks 020 7364 7971
Free www.towerhamlets.gov.uk/default.aspx?page=12670
Open Daily 7am–dusk
Tube Mile End **Train** Cambridge Heath **Bus** 8, 277, 339, 388, 425
Excellent access and facilities for wheelchair users

If you appreciate quietness, it's probably not a good idea to visit during one of the free music festivals held here in the summer, but at other times this peaceful park is not only one of the largest in London, it is also the oldest. Frequently awarded Green Flag status, this 170-year-old park borders the Hertford Union Canal, from where you can walk to Camden and beyond. The lake is very tranquil and watching the swans glide on the water can be very calming. In the early evening, long shadows form across the grass, giving striking, slowly changing views as people gradually pick themselves up from sitting on the grass and wend their way home.

Thames Barrier Park

North Woolwich Road, E16 2HP ☎ 020 7476 3741
Free www.london.gov.uk/priorities/housing-land/land-assets/thames-barrier-park
Open All day every day
DLR Pontoon Dock **Bus** 474
The park is wheelchair accessible

The first tree in this serene 22-acre park down by the Thames Barrier was planted in 1998 and the entrancing gardens were opened two years later to great acclaim. The plants have beautifully matured since then, and huge white hydrangea blossoms float like small clouds among the tall, wave-like green hedges. The Green Dock has an Alice in Wonderland feel – with its long, undulating box borders you can hide from view and appear as if from nowhere behind the next hedge. There are many different vistas, from the simple walkways above to dramatic views of the riverside. From its wildflower meadows to the views of the massive barrier, this award-winning green space is a precious oasis by the Thames.

Epping Forest

Epping Forest Visitor Centre, High Beach IG10 4AE ☎ 020 8508 0028
Free www.cityoflondon.gov.uk/things-to-do/green-spaces/epping-forest
Open All day, every day. Visitor Centre weekends and Bank Holidays 10am–3pm
Tube Buckhurst Hill **Train** Chingford or Loughton then bus 250, 255, 444 **Bus** 179, 397
See the website for details of the four purpose-built easy access paths at High Beach,
Connaught Water, Knighton Wood and Jubilee Pond

Epping Forest is London's largest open space and walking past the venerable, aged
oaks, it also feels like one of its most ancient places. The forest has hardly changed
since Tudor times, and with over 21 kilometres of open woodland, from Manor Park to
Essex, there is plenty to explore. Two thirds of the forest have been designated a Site
of Special Scientific Interest where around 500 rare species thrive. Look up to marvel
at the ancient pollarded oaks, beech and hornbeams, and down at the forest floor
to find red, white and yellow fungi among the leaf mould. The oak polypore and the
zoned rosette are especially rare in Western Europe but this is one place where you
can find them. Do remember, though, that visitors aren't allowed to pick fungi here.

Wimbledon Common

The Parkside, Wimbledon SW19 4UE, entrances also on Windmill Road, Calonne Road, Kingston Road, Barham Road and Parkside among others
☎ Ranger's Office 020 8788 7655
www.wpcc.org.uk, www.wimbledonwindmill.org.uk
Free but there is an entrance fee for the Windmill Museum, open April–October
Open All day every day **Tube** and **Train** Wimbledon **Bus** 57, 93, 200
Many paths are wheelchair accessible in dry weather

This large West London common is an invigorating space to walk, whether you are exercising your dog or encouraging your children to run free outdoors. With 1,140 acres of wilderness split between Wimbledon Common, Putney Heath and Putney Lower Common, there is enough open space for everyone to wander peacefully here. Come and see bluebells around the Fishponds Nature Reserve in spring, mauve heather on the heath in late summer, and walk through sparse woodland in the wintry months. Birdwatchers flock to the nine ponds to see greylag geese, egrets and grebes while anyone interested in the history of the commons can visit the former windmill, now a small museum run by volunteers.

Mitcham Common

Windmill Road, Mitcham CR4 1HT ☎ Warden's Office 020 8288 0453 **Free**
Open All day every day
Train Mitcham Eastfields **Tramlink** Mitcham Junction **Bus** 118, 264
The paths are wheelchair accessible in dry weather

Part of the Wandle Valley Country Park, these untamed 460 hilly acres on the edge of London feel as if they have remained undisturbed for centuries. In the middle of the common, the calm Seven Islands pond attracts swans and other wild birds, such as chiffchaffs and kingfishers. The acid grassland offers the ideal habitat for gorse, as well as being a refuge for marsh orchids and many wild creatures. Insects that thrive here include striped winged grasshoppers, damselflies and the common blue butterfly. In early autumn, the brambles are heavy with plump blackberries, enticing jam makers to gather wild fruit to make luscious preserves.

Cohen's Fields

Entrance opposite 26 Hampstead Lane, N6 4NX
Free www.hampsteadheath.net/cohen-s-fields.html
Open All day every day
Tube Highgate **Bus** 210, 214, 603
Wheelchair access possible during dry weather, but the footpaths can be steep and stony

Thousands of Londoners visit Hampstead Heath every year, but few know of the dramatic paths through Cohen's Fields on its north-eastern border. Named after a member of the Kenwood Preservation Society, these meadows are both secret and yet spectacular open spaces. Walking through the two fields is like finding yourself in the middle of the countryside instead of built-up North London. Each grassy rise is surrounded by thick, dense hedges and, like a series of windswept rooms, they lead you on, curious to discover what lies beyond the next hill. The upper field has some ancient oaks alongside the southern footpath while the lower field ends up at Stock Pond, a hidden pool surrounded by a tangle of trees.

Sydenham Hill Wood

Entrances on Sydenham Hill, Cox's Walk, Crescent Wood Road, Forest Hill, SE26
☎ 020 7525 2000
Free www.southwark.gov.uk/info/461/a_to_z_of_parks/670/sydenham_hill_wood/1
Open All day every day
Train Forest Hill **Bus** 63, 176, 185, 197, 363, 356, P4
There is no wheelchair access from the Cox's Walk entrance, and many uneven steps
in the woodland

Sydenham Woods is a marvellous anachronism – an ancient wood which still survives
in a hilly suburb on the borders of Forest Hill. You can stand on the footbridge where
Camille Pissarro painted his *Lordship Lane Station, Dulwich* in 1871, although nature
has entirely reclaimed the view in the last hundred years. Underneath the bridge the
former railway line has been converted into a wide path. Walking here surrounded
by tall oaks and beech trees, this verdant ravine feels miles away from the urban
landscape of South London.

Queen's Wood

Between Muswell Hill Road, Onslow Gardens, Connaught Gardens, Queen's Wood Road and Priory Gardens, N10 3JP
Free www.fqw.org.uk **Open** All day every day
Tube Highgate **Bus** 43, 134
The paths near Muswell Hill Road are accessible

This ancient woodland dates from at least 1600 and was renamed Queen's Wood in the 1890s during Victoria's reign. A local nature reserve, the wood has been awarded the highest grading as a Site of Metropolitan Importance by the London Ecology Unit. This is a magical place to go for a walk at any time during the year. Surrounded by ancient oaks and hornbeams for as far as you can see, it's easy to forget you are still in London. Not only is this an excellent place to see wild flowers such as wood sorrel, wild anemones, bluebells, dog violets and buttercups, but you can also spot ground-feeding birds such as song thrushes and even birds of prey such as sparrowhawks. The organic café near Muswell Hill Road plays background music, but on Friday evenings you can join in a gentle sound meditation with Tibetan singing bowls.

King Henry's Walk Garden

11c King Henry's Walk, Islington N1 4NX ☎ 020 7923 9035
Free www.khwgarden.org.uk **Open** Saturday and Sunday 12–4pm
Train Canonbury, Dalston Kingsland, Dalston Junction
Bus 21, 30, 38, 56, 277, 141
The garden is wheelchair accessible. Only registered assistance dogs are allowed in

King Henry's Walk Garden, an award-winning green space on the edge of Islington, was created in 2007 by the local community for local people. It is much appreciated by both the gardeners who tend their plots and anyone who comes to admire their green-fingered efforts. Here, the emphasis is on using organic gardening methods, mainly to attract wildlife and encourage biodiversity. With a profusion of over 45 flowering and leafy plants, including fuchsias, teasels, dahlias, alliums, euphorbias, tulips and geraniums, there are many blooms to admire throughout the year. Run by enthusiastic volunteers, this entrancing garden is a haven not only for birds, bees and butterflies, but for anyone who comes here to appreciate its quiet delights.

Churchyards & cemeteries

Walthamstow Cemetery
Queens Road, E17 8QP ☎ 020 8524 5030
Free www.walthamforest.gov.uk/pages/servicechild/walthamstow-cemetery-queens-road.aspx
Open Monday–Saturday 7.30am–4pm, Sunday 10am–4pm November–March,
Monday–Saturday 7.30am–7.30pm, Sunday 10am–6pm April October
Train Queen's Road **Bus** 58, 158
The cemetery is wheelchair accessible

This municipal cemetery opened in 1871, and most of the headstones in front of the Victorian buildings are from this era. It is probably not worth making a long trip from central London to come here, but if you are in the area it is a fascinating way to learn about local history from the carved inscriptions on the tombstones. Near the two chapels and the belfry are some thriving holly trees and other evergreens which offer welcome shade on hot summer days.

Abney Park

Stoke Newington High Street, N16 0LH, second entrance on Stoke Newington
Church Street ☎ 020 7275 7557 **Free** www.abneypark.org
Open Daily 8am–7pm summer, 8am–5pm October, 8am–4pm winter
Visitor centre Monday–Friday 9.30am–5pm
Train Stoke Newington **Bus** 67, 73, 76, 106, 149, 243, 276, 393, 476
Abney Park is wheelchair accessible in dry weather

Abney Park in Stoke Newington used to be Hackney's main cemetery until it was
turned into a woodland memorial park and local nature reserve. Planted in the
1840s as an arboretum, the park is managed by the Abney Park Trust, who allow the
undergrowth to flourish, giving the area a wild, untamed look. Common hawthorn,
Bhutan pine and other tall trees are overgrown with tousled ivy and other climbing
plants – the perfect surroundings for native species to flourish. It is easy to get lost
and forget you are in the middle of Hackney. At dusk, owls can be heard hooting and
bats start their nightly ventures, maybe swooping down over the headstone of William
Booth, founder of the Salvation Army, who is buried here.

Old St Mary's Church, Stoke Newington

Stoke Newington Church Street, N16 9ES ☎ 020 7254 6072
Free www.stmaryn16.org
Open All day every day, church Tuesday–Friday 9am–5pm
Train Stoke Newington **Bus** 73, 393, 476
There is wheelchair access along the paths but they can be uneven

This ancient churchyard can be found in a quiet corner of Stoke Newington close to
Clissold Park. With its majestic chestnut trees and low rectangular stone tombs, the
pretty graveyard has a calm atmosphere reminiscent of rural parishes. A number of
Abolitionists are buried in the churchyard, and the author Daniel Defoe lived in the
same street. Now mainly used as an arts centre, the church organises an annual arts
festival, where local people gather together to view art, debate ideas and listen to
music. This is a good opportunity to learn more about the history of the building and
the people who live and work in the vicinity.

All Saints Poplar
Newby Place, E14 0EY ☎ 020 7538 9198 **Free**
Open Daily 9am–5pm
DLR All Saints **Bus** 309, D6
The churchyard has wheelchair access

Describing itself as a place of calm, peace and safety, this East End church is a
welcoming haven in this deprived area of London. A Grade II-listed building, All Saints
was built from granite and Portland stone by Thomas Morris, a local builder whose
grave can be seen just north of the church door in the churchyard. Completed in
1823, the church was badly damaged in the Second World War and the crypt probably
wasn't the safest place to take shelter during the bombings. Not far from Canary
Wharf, this quiet green space now offers a welcome breathing space in an area with
few gardens.

St Paul's Churchyard, Deptford

Diamond Way, off Deptford High Street, Deptford SE8 3DS
☎ 020 8692 7449 **Free**
Open Daily 9am–dusk
DLR Deptford Bridge **Train** Deptford, New Cross **Bus** 47, 53, 177, 188, 199
The churchyard is wheelchair accessible

It is a real surprise to find this magnificent 1730s, Grade I-listed Queen Anne church
in a pretty churchyard just off Deptford High Street. With its unusual cylindrical tower
and elegant steeple, this is one of the architectural highlights of South London.
Typical of many ecclesiastical eighteenth-century buildings, the church is constructed
from Portland stone but it has some spectacular Tuscan columns around its base.
Whatever direction you approach from, the views of the churchyard are uplifting. From
winter mornings with frost on the trees to autumn afternoons when the leaves turn
bronze and gold, this is a lovely place to go for a walk.

St Nicholas's Churchyard, Deptford

Deptford Green, SE8 3DQ ☎ 020 8692 2749
www.deptfordchurch.org
Open All day every day, church Wednesday–Saturday 9.30am–12.30pm, Sunday 9am–12pm
DLR Deptford Bridge **Train** Deptford **Bus** 47, 53, 177, 188, 199
The church and churchyard are wheelchair accessible

The original name for this area was Depeford, suggesting that many years ago there was a deep ford crossing in the vicinity. Located close to the River Thames, this ancient church occupies a quiet corner of the city, and the churchyard is a delightful place to walk through. This historic site has associations with the poet and playwright Christopher Marlowe who died in 1593. He is buried in an unmarked grave, but his memorial plaque can be found on the wall of the churchyard.

St Mary's Churchyard, Barnes

Church Road, Barnes SW13 9HL ☎ 020 8741 5422
Free www.stmarybarnes.org
Open All day every day, church Monday–Friday 10.30am–12.30pm and during services
Train Barnes **Bus** 33, 72, 209, 283, 485
The church and churchyard are wheelchair accessible

St Mary's Church is the oldest building in the parish of Barnes. It was constructed of coursed flint between 1100 and 1150 and enlarged in 1215 after the signing of the Magna Carta. It suffered a massive fire in the early 1980s, after which the nave and ceiling were rebuilt. This Grade II-listed building not only has an architecturally impressive modern timber ceiling, it also has an ancient side chapel and a pretty churchyard. It almost feels as if you are in the countryside, walking along the flint paths among the headstones. The church also has a strong choral tradition, and hosts excellent concerts during the annual Barnes music festival.

St George the Martyr Church Gardens

Tabard Street, SE1 IJA ☎ 0207 357 0331 (but email is preferable,
admin@stgeorge-themartyr.co.uk) **Free** www.stgeorge-themartyr.co.uk
Open Daily 9am–dusk
Tube Borough **Bus** 21, 35, 40, 133, 343, C10,
The gardens are wheelchair accessible

The church of St George the Martyr is associated with Charles Dickens, whose
father was imprisoned for debt in the Marshalsea Prison. The site of the prison was
just beyond the far wall of the garden – an Historic Southwark plaque can be seen
noting this biographical detail. The buildings surrounding this former churchyard are
covered with ivy, an old-fashioned example of a 'living wall'. In spring, flowering bulbs
display their colourful petals under tall plane trees, and to the left of the entrance
there's a rockery of small-leaved plants to admire, making this a pleasant place to
sit on sunny mornings.

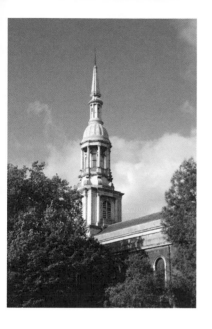

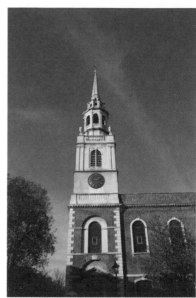

St Leonard's Churchyard Gardens

Shoreditch High Street, E1 6JN
☎ 020 7739 2063 **Free**
www.shoreditchchurch.wordpress.com
Open Daily dawn–dusk, church Monday–Friday 12–2pm **Tube** Old Street **Train** Shoreditch High Street **Bus** 24, 26, 35, 47, 48, 55, 67, 78, 135, 149, 242
The gardens are wheelchair accessible

George Dance the Elder designed this beautiful church after the previous one collapsed when its foundations flooded in the eighteenth century. Elizabethan actors are buried in the twelfth-century crypt, while the exterior garden is a haven for wildlife.

St James Clerkenwell

Clerkenwell Close, EC1R 0EA
☎ 020 7251 1190 **Free** www.jc-church.org
Open Usually Monday–Friday 9.30am–5.30pm, Sunday service 11am
Tube Farringdon, Angel **Bus** 55, 153, 243
The church and churchyard are both wheelchair accessible

With its huge plane trees and handsome church spire, this must be one of the prettiest churchyards in London. The church interior has pale blue and white plaster cornice decoration on the ceiling, like a Wedgwood plate turned upside down.

St Mary's Church and Churchyard, Walthamstow

8 Church End, Walthamstow E17 9RJ ☎ 020 8520 1430
Free www.walthamstowchurch.org.uk
Open Churchyard all day every day, to visit the church call for an appointment
Tube Walthamstow Central **Bus** 212
Church End path next to the churchyard is wheelchair accessible

For anyone outside the area, Walthamstow Village comes as a bit of a surprise.
Opposite the pebbledashed church is a fifteenth-century timber-framed house and
the nearby streets look like a model English village. The churchyard is the most rural
part of this conservation area, and squirrels can be seen running up and down trees,
oblivious to the comings and goings of local people walking down the church path.
The area is changing rapidly, with new restaurants and shops opening every week,
yet this attractive churchyard remains as tranquil as ever.

St Giles-in-the-Fields Churchyard

60 St Giles High Street, WC2H 8LG ☎ 0207 240 2532
Free www.stgilesonline.org
Open Daily dawn–dusk, church Monday–Friday 9am–5pm
Tube Tottenham Court Road **Bus** 1, 8, 19, 24, 29, 38, 55, 134, 176, 242, 390
The church and churchyard are both wheelchair accessible

There has been a Christian presence on this site since 1101, when Queen Matilda
founded a leper hospital in St Giles. This crowded district of London also has a
nefarious past, renowned for debauchery, thievery and squalor in the eighteenth
century – the artist William Hogarth illustrated the area in *Gin Lane*. The present
church was built in 1730, and the children of Byron and of Percy Bysshe and Mary
Shelley were all baptised here. The church interior is sober and restrained, with
dark wood pews and simple white walls. The large garden behind the church is
now a peaceful place where local people come to sit and or walk their dogs.

St George-in-the-East Church
14 Cannon Street Road, E1 0BH, entrances on Cable Street and The Highway
☎ Church 020 7481 1345, Tower Hamlets parks 020 7364 6673
Free www.stgite.org.uk, www.towerhamlets.gov.uk/lgsl/451-500/461_parks/st_
georges_gardens.aspx **Open** Churchyard daily dawn–dusk
DLR Shadwell **Bus** 100, D3
The church is not wheelchair accessible but the surrounding gardens do have access

When the founder of Methodism, John Wesley, preached here, the area known as Wapping-Stepney was still quite rural. Built in 1729, this rather grand church was badly damaged during the bombing raids of 1941 and it wasn't until 1964 that a new, inner church was built inside the ruins. The exterior walls still stand, however, and Hawksmoor's towers loom over the surrounding area. It is worth coming here to see both the modernist ecclesiastical architecture and to amble in the walled churchyard. Part of the St George-in-the-East Conservation Area, the spacious grass lawn is also a great place to go for early morning walks.

St Mary's Churchyard, Bermondsey

193 Bermondsey Street, SE1 3UW, at the corner of Abbey Street and Tower Bridge Road ☎ 020 7357 0984
Free www.stmarysbermondsey.org.uk/the-churchyard-memorials/
Open All day every day
Tube Bermondsey, Borough, London Bridge **Bus** 42, 78, 188, C10
The churchyard is wheelchair accessible

A church has existed close to this site since 1290, when St Mary Magdalen Chapel was first recorded in the area known as Bermondsey. This attractive churchyard can be found at the corner of two main roads, but it still seems to be a very peaceful place. Families come here to picnic or sit on the grass with their children, often after buying lunch at the nearby Saturday farmers' market on Bermondsey Square. As well as a few eighteenth-century tombs, in the middle of the green open space is an unusual drinking fountain – a late Gothic revival edifice made in 1902 of limestone and pink granite.

St Paul's Churchyard, Shadwell

302 The Highway, E1W 3DH ☎ 020 7680 2772
Free www.stpaulsshadwell.org
Open Daily 8am–6pm
Tube Shadwell, Wapping **DLR** Shadwell **Bus** 100, D3
The churchyard is wheelchair accessible

Built in 1657, St Paul's is a fine-looking Grade II-listed church near the peaceful
Shadwell Basin. Captain James Cook used to attend services here before travelling to
the South Seas. Although the church is on the main road, the leafy garden behind is
unexpectedly peaceful. This feels like a very private corner, and the wooden benches
are a great place to read or just sit and listen to the birds. With a fine view of the
church steeple and overhanging trees, this quiet enclave offers respite from the
often uninspiring surroundings of the East End.

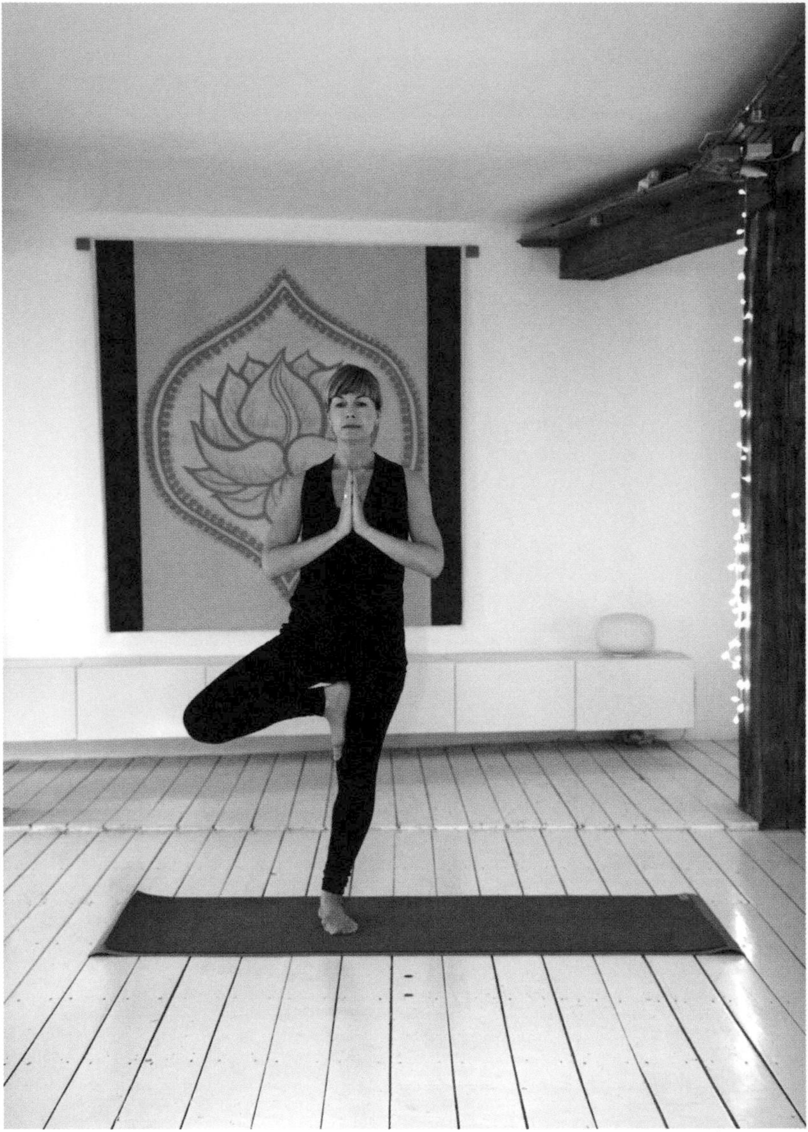

Places to relax

Reva Yoga

2c Andrews Road, Broadway Market, E8 4QL ☎ 07917 360 741
£ www.revayoga.com
Open Saturday classes 10.30am–12pm, open to everyone (for other classes see website), closed Bank Holidays, over Christmas and for a few weeks in summer
Tube Bethnal Green **Train** Cambridge Heath, Haggerston **Bus** 48, 394
There is no wheelchair access to the yoga studio

From baby yoga classes, which strengthen the bonds between parent and child, to the popular Saturday morning yoga sessions, this is a very restful place to practise asanas and breathing exercises. Satyananda Yoga Teacher Nina Deeley trained in India and she inspires everyone with her guided meditations in a beautiful converted loft just off Broadway Market. Satyananda Yoga encourages a deeply spiritual approach and enables people to develop an inner state of harmony – it is suitable for everyone, both young and old.

Neal's Yard Remedies Therapy Rooms

2 Neal's Yard, Covent Garden WC2H 9DP
☎ 020 7379 7662
£ www.nealsyardremedies.com
Open Monday–Thursday 9am–9pm, Friday 9am–7pm, Saturday and Sunday 10am–6.30pm **Tube** Covent Garden, Tottenham Court Road **Bus** 1, 8, 19, 24, 29, 38, 55, 134, 176, 242, 390
Not wheelchair accessible

The revered health and beauty products company Neal's Yard Remedies started in this courtyard. They offer Reiki massage, osteopathy and other therapies in the small treatment rooms in this former warehouse.

London Natural Health

46 Theobald's Road, WC1X 8NW
☎ 020 7242 6665
£ www.londonnatural.co.uk
Open Monday–Friday 9am–9pm, Saturday and Sunday by appointment
Tube Holborn **Bus** 19, 38, 55, 243
The centre is not wheelchair accessible

With over eighty practitioners and 108 therapies, it would be hard not to find something to help you feel calmer after a session here. Try an excellent sports massage or reflexology for tired feet and aching limbs. Nutritional supplements are offered for sale at reception.

Amber Beauty Salon

Seymour Leisure Centre, Seymour Place, W1H 5TJ ☎ 0207 724 2800
£ www.amberbeautysalon.co.uk
Open Tuesday–Thursday 10am–8pm, Friday 10am–7pm, Saturday 10am–6pm, Sunday
10am–5pm, closed Monday and Bank Holidays
Tube Baker Street, Edgware Road, Marylebone **Bus** 2, 18, 27, 205, 453
The beauty salon is not wheelchair accessible

Patsy Braham has been offering rejuvenating facials, beauty treatments and
reflexology at this small salon inside the Seymour Leisure Centre for many years.
She has a loyal following among her numerous clients, due to the fact that she makes
everyone feel really pampered and cared for. She will gently massage stiff shoulders
and furrowed brows using Guinot and other superlative treatments. For one hour you
don't have to do anything at all but allow her soothing touch to make you feel ten
years younger.

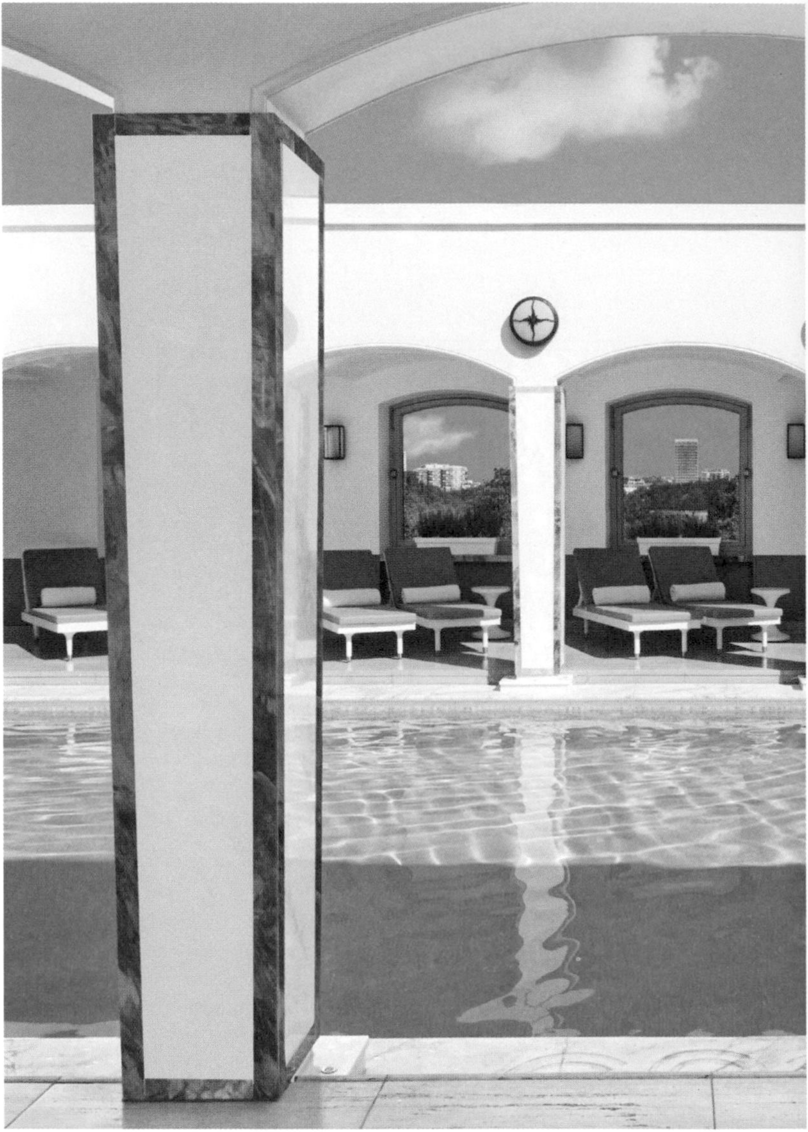

Bamford Haybarn at The Berkeley

Wilton Place, Knightsbridge SW1X 7RL ☎ 020 7201 1699
£ www.the-berkeley.co.uk
Open Monday–Friday 6am–10pm, Saturday and Sunday 7am–9pm, treatments available daily 9am–7pm, no children in the pool after 7pm
Tube Knightsbridge, Hyde Park Corner **Bus** 14, 22, 38, 74, 414, C1
Wheelchair accessible via rear entrance and lift to 8th floor, no accessible toilets

The Haybarn sounds rustic but only a few signs of the countryside are evident in this luxury rooftop health club and spa. The towel hooks are made from holly branches from Dayesford Farm and their herbs provide scents for the organic potions and balms sold in the small shop. This is a sophisticated oasis to find respite from the city down below. The tranquil pool is surrounded by white loungers and you can spend hours here reading a book while looking up at the sky – the roof can be opened in summer. You can also enjoy The Berkeley's beautifully prepared cuisine here, as the light meals offered by the poolside are delicious and the wine list is excellent. After a languid swim, relax in the Finnish sauna and steam rooms. At the end of the day, this is the perfect place to meet up with a quiet friend for some peaceful pampering.

Hair by Georgina

Home visits by appointment (her home, near Clapham Junction, or yours)
☎ 07738 877 139
£ www.hairbygeorgina.co.uk
Open Flexible times

Georgina has been a professional hairdresser for many years, and now offers haircuts and colour treatments away from noisy salons. She is expert at bridal hairstyles, and can travel outside London for special occasions. With no salon overheads, her prices are very reasonable. If you have always wanted to have your hair cut in a quiet garden surrounded by birdsong, she is very happy to fulfil your wishes.

Naiobicrafts and Complementary Therapies

Unit 5, 100 Wood Street, E17 3HX
☎ 07757 742 305
£ www.naiobicrafts.co.uk
Open Wednesday–Sunday from 7am, by appointment only
Tube Walthamstow Central **Train** Wood Street **Bus** 20, 123, 212, 230, 275, W16
The massage room is accessible with just a 3cm step to enter

Tucked inside the Georgian Village, Enitan offers superb facials and back massage using Neal's Yard Remedies oils. Her sense of humour is relaxing in itself and she knows how to soothe stressed bodies and troubled minds.

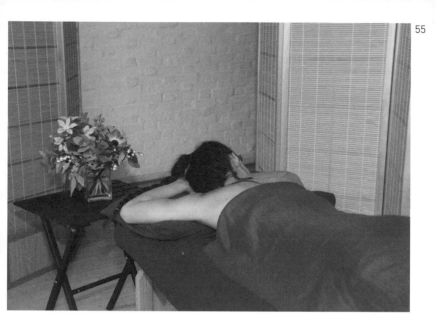

Holistic Health Hackney

64 Broadway Market, E8 4QJ ☎ 020 7275 8434
£ www.holistichealthhackney.co.uk
Open Daily 9am to late, including Christmas Day and New Year's Day
Tube Bethnal Green **Train** London Fields **Bus** 26, 48, 236, 254, 388, 394, D6
There are three rooms on the ground floor with wide door access and accessible toilet facilities

This welcoming holistic health centre was set up by enterprising podiatrist Tracey Byrne over six years ago – with over fifty practitioners and thirty therapies, it offers one of the widest range of mainstream and alternative treatments in London. From Thai massage to Bowen technique, osteopathy and naturopathy, there will always be someone in this multidisciplinary practice to help you find your inner balance. Although most of the therapies are body-oriented, the centre also offers hypnotherapy and counselling, where emotional stress can be remedied with patient listening.

56

The School of Meditation

158 Holland Park Avenue, W11 4UH ☎ 020 7603 6116
£ donations on a sliding scale, depending on income
www.schoolofmeditation.org
Open 1st Thursday and 3rd Sunday of the month open evenings when anyone can
enrol on a course, closed Bank Holidays, August and over Christmas
Tube Holland Park **Bus** 31, 94, 148, 228, 295, 316
There are numerous steps into the house but once inside there are accessible toilets

The School of Meditation was founded in 1959 during the Maharishi's first visit to
London, as a place for individuals to learn meditation from the ancient Vedic tradition.
Silent mantra practice usually takes place in small groups, but one-to-one sessions
can also be arranged. In this peaceful Georgian house in West London anyone
is welcome, whatever their philosophical or religious background. As well as an
enlightening ten-week philosophy group, one of the most important aspects of the
school is the personal care offered to participants.

Mei Quan Academy of Tai Chi

Charles Dickens Primary School,
Toulmin Street, Borough SE1 1AF
☎ Stephen Holder 07799 038 016
£ www.taichinews.com
Open Classes Wednesday 7pm, but
subject to change so check in advance
Tube Borough **Bus** 35, 40, 133, 343, C10
The school is not wheelchair accessible

The Charles Dickens School is just
one of the many places where you can
practice the Mei Quan approach to Tai
Chi. From Camberwell to Crouch End,
the Mei Quan Academy runs many
classes throughout London and has
38 locations to choose from.

Mary Ward Centre Tai Chi

10 Great Turnstile, WC1V 7JU
☎ 020 7831 7079 £ www.maryward
centre.ac.uk/courses/subject/tai-chi
Open Classes Monday, book in advance
for a series **Tube** Holborn, Chancery
Lane **Bus** 1, 8, 19, 25, 55, 59, 68, 91, 98,
168, 171, 188, 242, 243, 521, X8
The centre is wheelchair accessible via
a platform lift

Tai Chi is probably one of the most
calming and restful of the activities
that go on here. Try out some graceful
moves during a daytime or evening
class, all of which are designed for
people of differing abilities.

Hinde Street Methodist Chapel

19 Thayer Street, W1U 2QJ ☎ 020 7935 6179
Free www.hindestreet.org.uk/hinde-street-weekly
Open Tuesday 1pm meditation in the Quiet Room
Tube Bond Street **Bus** 2, 7, 8, 10, 13, 25, 30, 55, 73, 74, 82, 98, 113, 139, 176, 189, 274, 390
There is no wheelchair access to the meditation room, only the main chapel. There is a street-level lift to main floors and toilets with wheelchair access

Every Tuesday lunchtime, anyone is welcome to join the weekly meditation group that meets in a quiet room inside one of London's prettiest Methodist chapels. If you aren't able to find quiet time during the working day, Hinde Street Chapel also organises talks on topics such as ethical responses to poverty and whether being wealthier in the West makes us happier. Discover more about the Hugh Price Lectures on their website, named after this revolutionary Victorian thinker and founder of the West London Mission.

West London Buddhist Centre

94 Westbourne Park Villas, W2 5EB ☎ 020 7727 9382
£ donation www.westlondonbuddhistcentre.com
Open Monday–Friday 1–2pm, Saturday 10am–12pm
Tube Westbourne Park, Royal Oak **Bus** 7, 23, 27, 36, 70
There is no wheelchair access to the meditation room

This small, friendly Buddhist centre offers weekday lunchtime meditation to anyone who wants to find some quiet time in their lives. Partly guided by an experienced leader, here it is easy to forget the fraught moments in our busy lives and just concentrate on simple breathing exercises and looking inwards. Instead of the internal chatter that keeps us preoccupied and distracted, meditating in this restful space is a good way to calm our 'monkey minds'.

The Hale Clinic
7 Park Crescent, W1B 1PF ☎ 020 7631 0156
£ www.haleclinic.com
Open Monday–Friday 8.30am–9pm, Saturday 9am–5pm, Friday 7pm drop in
for 'Om healing', private classes also available
Tube Regent's Park, Great Portland Street **Train** Marylebone, Euston, King's Cross
Bus 88, 453, C28
The ground floor is accessible and there is a lift but a special chair is needed upstairs

Some people might assume that this clinic, close to Regent's Park, is only frequented
by the wealthy and exquisitely groomed. The staff welcome anyone, however, and
people from all different walks of life come here. The centre is run by Teresa Hale,
who began teaching meditation and yoga over thirty years ago. She is expert at
teaching anyone how to find stillness within themselves, so that even when they are
in stressful situations they are not disturbed by unwanted noise. Her small group
sessions mean that everyone gets individual attention in their search for inner peace.

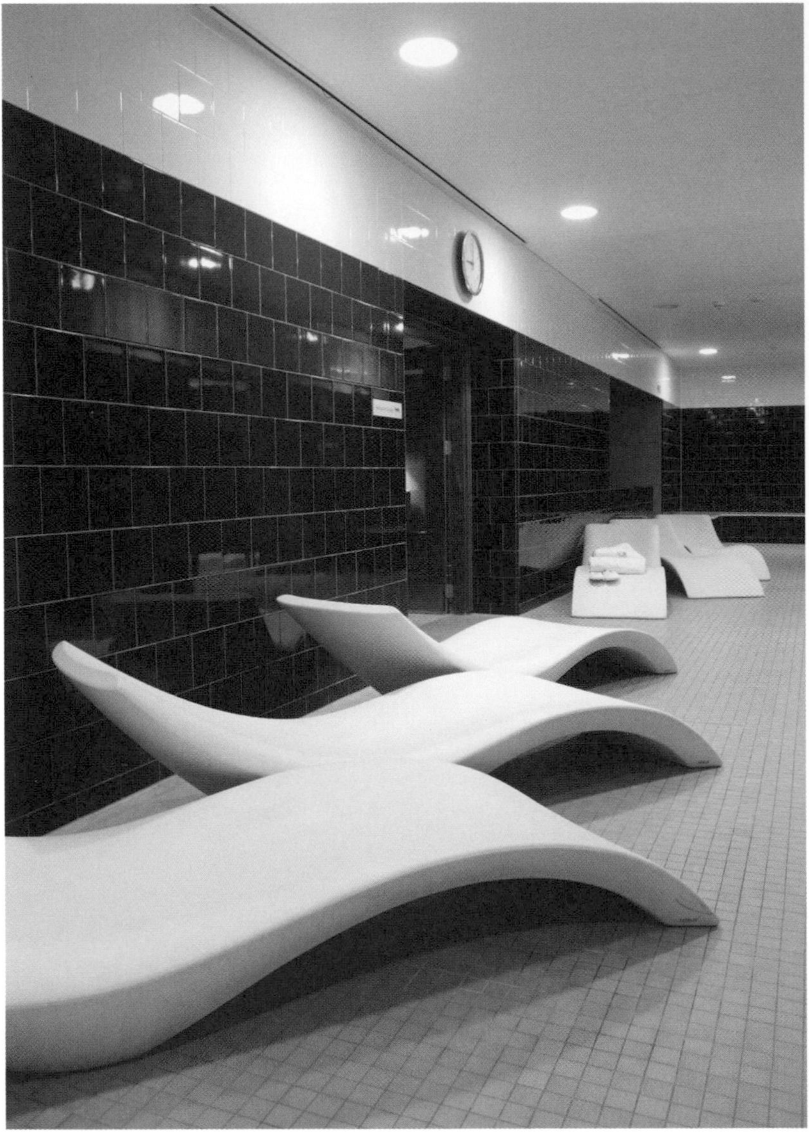

Ironmonger Row Spa

Ironmonger Row, 1 Norman Street, EC1V 3AA ☎ 020 3642 5521
£ www.spa-london.org/ironmonger-row-baths
Open Monday 11am–9pm, Tuesday–Friday 10am–9pm, Saturday and Sunday 9am–6pm
Women only Monday to 6pm, Thursday and Friday to 5.30pm; men only Tuesday and
Thursday 6–9pm; all other times mixed
Tube Old Street **Bus** 4, 43, 55, 56, 205, 214, 243, 394
Adapted for wheelchairs, with accessible changing rooms and toilets, induction loop,
ramp access and lift

Ironmonger Row Baths is an East London Institution and used to be the local bath
house for working people in the area. A few years ago the Turkish baths were totally
refurbished and transformed into an upmarket spa. The Tepidarium and Caldarium
warm, dry-air rooms are still here, and lying on the hot stones is an excellent way
to recuperate after a long day. Sit wrapped in a towel in the sauna, then smother
yourself with ice flakes and linger in the citrus aroma steam room. End your stay with
a dip in the hydrotherapy pool then take a quiet nap in the relaxation area, lying down
like Cleopatra in her bedchamber.

City Lit

Keeley Street, Covent Garden WC2B 4BA

☎ switchboard 020 7492 2600, enrolments 020 7831 7831

£ www.citylit.ac.uk/courses

Open During term times with classes

Tube Holborn, Covent Garden

Bus 1, 8, 19, 25, 38, 55, 59, 68, 91, 168, 171, 188, 242, 243, 521, X68

The City Lit is wheelchair accessible, with specialist courses for deaf and hard-of-hearing students

From chi kung to Pilates classes where you can learn gentle breathing techniques, there are many courses to help you relax and look after your body at this popular inner city college. One of the most interesting is 'Sunday life drawing; experimental approaches', a four-week course which involves doing warm-up exercises as well as learning about observational drawing. Using a range of media and techniques, including mindfulness strategies derived from meditation, this is an innovative way to approach the figure. Most courses at City Lit run over a few weeks, but prospective students can also enrol on one-day taster sessions.

Kieser Training

Greater London House, Hampstead Road, NW1 7DF ☎ 020 7391 9980
www.kieser-training.co.uk
Open Monday–Friday 7–9.30am, weekends and public holidays 9am–6pm
Tube Mornington Crescent **Bus** 24, 29, 88, 134, 168, 214, 253, 476
No wheelchair access

Kieser Training is unlike any other fitness centre in Britain. Instead of loud music
and a hyped-up atmosphere, the specialist programme offered here is more like a
supervised but independent series of exercises. An on-site doctor will approve your
training programme and qualified instructors introduce you to each machine, working
out the ideal body strengthening exercises to overcome injury or improve strength and
flexibility. The influence of the Bauhaus is everywhere, from the Swiss railway clocks
on the wall to the simple design of the large, sunlit space. This is the quietest centre
to improve your fitness in London.

Yoga Mama

The Putney Clinic, 266 Upper Richmond Road, SW15 6TQ ☎ 020 8789 3881
£ www.putneyclinic.co.uk
Open Monday–Friday, see website for current timetable
Tube East Putney, Putney **Bus** 14, 39, 74 ,85, 93, 220, 265, 270, 337, 414, 424, 430 485
The yoga room and toilet facilities are wheelchair accessible

Cherie Lathey is a well-qualified teacher who runs yoga and Pilates classes in this sunny room in the centre of Putney. Located on the first floor of a health centre, her holistic classes perfectly complement the allopathic treatments in the GP surgery below. As well as ashtanga, hatha, prenatal and mother and baby yoga, remedial and postnatal Pilates are also offered. If you feel really stressed, follow her dynamic yoga session with a specially tailored retreat in this more rural part of London.

Westminster Physiotherapy & Pilates Centre

Lower Grosvenor Place, SW1W 0EN
☎ 020 7834 3700
www.westminsterphysio.co.uk
Open Monday–Friday 8am–8pm
Tube Victoria **Bus** 2, 24, 38, 52, 73, 211, 38, 436, C10
There is a small step at the front door and ground floor treatment rooms, and no access to the downstairs toilet

Even if you don't have an injury, it is worth coming here for the attentive Pilates sessions held in the well-equipped rear studio. In very small classes, qualified physiotherapists help us be more aware of our bodies.

Age Exchange

Centre for Reminiscence Arts,
Blackheath SE3 9LA ☎ 020 8318 9105
£ www.age-exchange.org.uk,
www.leegreenlives.org.uk/taichi.htm
Open Friday 12.30–1.30pm
Train Blackheath **Bus** 54, 89, 108, 202
The centre has wheelchair access

Although the excellent Tai Chi class at Age Exchange is run solely for people over sixty, tutor Stelios Lambis also gives lessons elsewhere in South London. This very experienced, calm teacher introduces the gentle moves of Tai Chi to people of all ages.

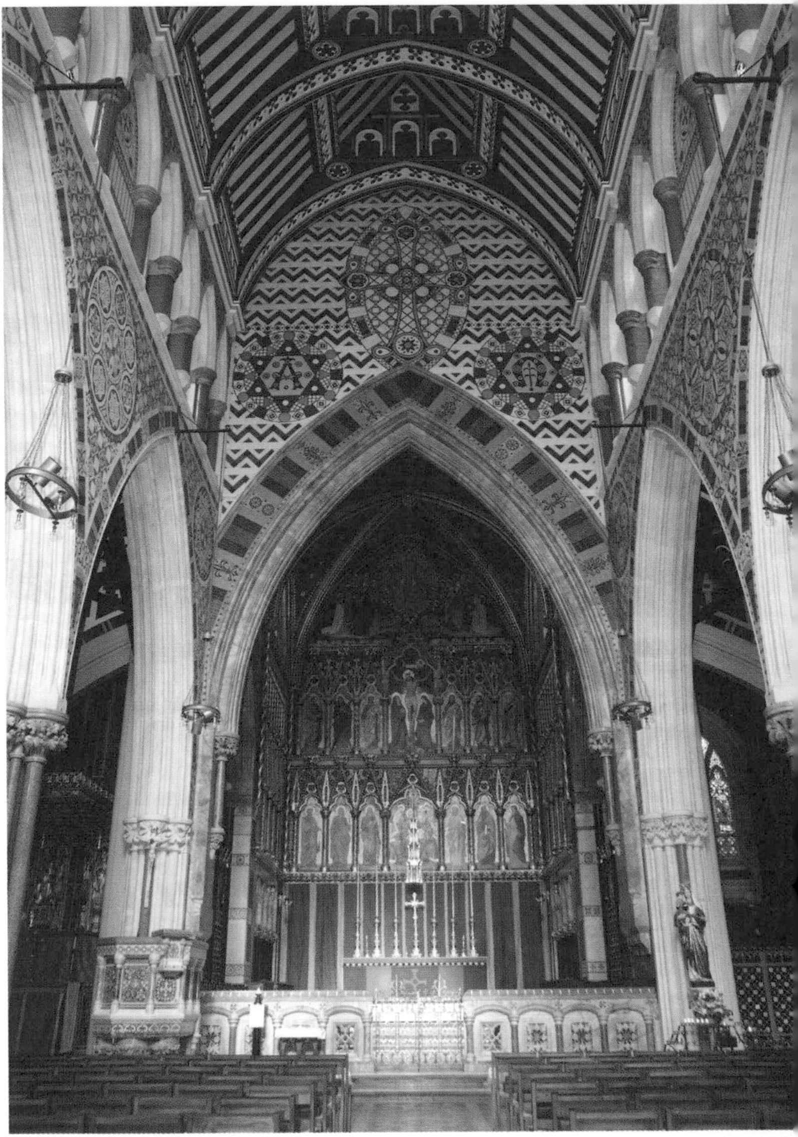

Places of worship

All Saints Margaret Street

Margaret Street, W1W 8JG ☎ 020 7636 1788
Free www.allsaintsmargaretstreet.org.uk
Open Daily 7am–7pm
Tube Oxford Circus, Goodge Street, Tottenham Court Road
Bus 7, 10, 73, 88, 98, 390, 453, C2
There are steps at the entrance but temporary ramps can be fitted on request and there are adapted toilets. A hearing loop has been installed

The extensive opening hours of this magnificent church are a testimony to its inclusiveness. Anyone can drop by to marvel at the extraordinary interior, or just sit quietly here. A Grade I-listed building, it was designed in the high Victorian gothic style by William Butterfield, and completed in 1859. The extravagant wall tiles were added later between 1873 and 1891 and decorate the walls around the nave. Huge panels painted by Alexander Gibbs illustrate early Christian saints and martyrs. Look out for the biblical scene of Moses holding up a serpent. The stained glass is dense with Christian narrative and it's also worth seeing Butterfield's intricate brass gates at the entrance to the chancel.

Newington Green Unitarians

39a Newington Green, Stoke Newington, N16 9PR ☎ 07809 144 879
Free but donations welcome www.new-unity.org
Open For Sunday service 11am, Tuesday meditation 7pm
Train Canonbury, Dalston Kingsland **Bus** 30, 73, 141, 236, 243, 341, 476
There is a ramp for wheelchair users at the rear of the church

This is the oldest Nonconformist chapel in London, purpose-built by Unitarians
in 1708. The feminist thinker Mary Wollstonecraft was an early member of the
congregation, living nearby in a house on Newington Green. Unlike most chapels,
you do not have to be a Christian believer to attend their Sunday morning services.
Instead, Unitarians describe themselves as a community of love, growth and social
justice. Many are atheists or sceptics, and their beliefs are closer to philosophy than
a religion so outside speakers are often invited to give talks here on subjects as varie
as compassionate communication and astronomy.

Golders Green Unitarians

31½ Hoop Lane, Golders Green NW11 8BS ☎ 020 8455 5000
Free www.ggu.org.uk
Open Services on Sunday, meditation 1st and 3rd Wednesday of the month 1.30pm
Tube Golders Green **Bus** 82, 102, 210, 460, H2
The chapel has wheelchair access but no adapted toilet

The opening words at their regular services say that the Unitarians are 'a church
without walls, open to mystery, responsive to need, with compassion and acceptance
for all'. This non-credal, non-orthodox church is also inspired by other world religions
and traditions. More universalist than other denominations, the Unitarians tend to
attract liberal, open-minded people who appreciate their eclectic vision. This building
also has another claim to fame – the painter Ivon Hitchens attended services in this
small chapel and his early, rather romantic mural in the tradition of Morris and Co.
still hangs on the walls of the semi-circular apse.

St Margaret Lothbury

Lothbury, EC2R 7HH ☎ 020 7726 4878
Free www.stml.org.uk
Open Daily 7am–6pm, closed Bank
Holidays, organ recitals Thursday 1pm
Tube Bank **Bus** 11, 23, 25, 26, 40, 76, 133,
242, 388
The church is wheelchair accessible

This exceptionally peaceful church
was designed by Sir Christopher Wren
and completed in 1692. The architect
Robert Hooke designed the tower, which
was added in 1700. Carved in 1684 for
another church, the intricate wooden
screen is a magnificent example of
English woodworking.

St George the Martyr

Borough High Street, SE1 IJA
☎ 0207 357 0331 (email preferable,
admin@stgeorge-themartyr.co.uk)
Free www.stgeorge-themartyr.co.uk
Open Thursday 9am–5pm or by
appointment **Tube** Borough
Bus 21, 35, 40, 133, 343, C10
The church is wheelchair accessible

Designed by the architect John Price
who died before he saw its completion
in 1736, this inner-city church is an
exceptional example of an early
eighteenth-century interior. Charles
Dickens had links with this church and
his character Little Dorrit is depicted
in a stained glass window.

St Mary Woolnoth

King William Street, London EC3V 9AN ☎ 020 7626 9701
Free www.stml.org.uk
Open Monday–Saturday 9am–7pm, weekday lunchtime services Wednesday and
Thursday, closed Sunday and Bank Holidays
Tube Bank **Bus** 11, 23, 25, 26, 40, 76, 133, 242, 388
The church is not wheelchair accessible

The sister church of St Margaret Lothbury, this small but beautifully proportioned
building is also an excellent example of baroque architecture with its ornate yet
restrained ecclesiastical interior. The only church in the City of London designed
by Nicholas Hawksmoor, it opened on Easter Day 1727. The interior is deceptively
spacious and, with its Corinthian columns and monumental exterior turrets,
the unusual design surprises even visitors who are familiar with City of London
churches. The Abolitionist William Wilberforce worshipped here, and the father of
the Elizabethan dramatist Thomas Kyd was churchwarden in the previous church
that stood on this site.

74

St Mary the Virgin

Upper Street, Islington N1 2TX ☎ 020 7226 3400
Free www.stmaryislington.org
Open Monday–Saturday 9.30am–4pm, Sunday 10am–7pm
Tube Angel, Highbury & Islington **Bus** 4, 30, 38, 43, 56, 73, 341
The church is wheelchair accessible

The first recorded vicar at St Mary's was Walter Gherkin in around 1300 and this thriving parish has had 51 vicars since the fourteenth century. Islington's main parish church, it was built in 1754 but bombed in the Blitz and largely rebuilt in 1956, although the strangely shaped obelisk spire and the crypt survived. The church has numerous claims to fame. George Wesley was expelled from the pulpit in 1739 for what some considered seditious preaching. The world's first black Anglican priest, West African Philip Quaque, was ordained here by the Bishop of London in 1765. Occasional Poetry in the Crypt readings held on Saturdays are among the highlights of the year, and a good way to raise money for charitable causes. On sunny days, as well as seeing light stream in through the church windows, it's nice to wander through St Mary's Gardens outside.

Blackheath Quaker Meeting

Friends Meeting House, Lawn Terrace,
Blackheath SE3 9LL ☎ 020 8852 7386,
07582 729 185 **Free** but donations
welcome for peace campaigns
www.quaker.org.uk/blackheath,
www.blackheathquakers.org.uk
Open Worship at 10.30am every Sunday
Train Blackheath **Bus** 54, 89, 108, 202
There is wheelchair access and a
hearing loop

This unusual 1960s meeting house won
an award from the Concrete Society for
its grey walls imprinted with planks. The
wooden ceiling and beautiful lantern
invite all who enter to look to the sky.

Jamyang Buddhist Centre

The Old Courthouse, 43 Renfrew Road,
SE11 4NA ☎ 020 7820 8787 **£** donation
www.jamyang.co.uk **Open** 10.30am–5pm,
silent meditation Thursday 6.15pm
Tube Kennington, Elephant & Castle
Bus 1, 3, 12, 35, 40, 45, 53, 59, 63, 68, 89,
109, 133, 148, 155, 159, 171, 172, 176, 188,
322, 333, 343, 344, 363, 453, 468, P5
The centre is accessible from the
garden entrance

A welcoming Buddhist centre where
you can learn Tai Chi, attend stress-
reduction classes, practise Satyananda
yoga or stay overnight on retreat in one
of the former police holding cells.

St Stephen Walbrook

39 Walbrook, EC4N 8BN ☎ 020 7626 9000
Free www.ststephenwalbrook.net, londoninternetchurch.org.uk
Open Monday–Friday 10am–4pm
Tube Bank **Bus** 8, 15, 21, 23, 25, 26, 43, 76, 141, 242
Ring the church in advance of your visit for wheelchair access

Designing this quite magnificent church enabled Sir Christopher Wren to try out some ideas he was to use in his plans for St Paul's Cathedral. Built on the site of a former church, this eighteenth-century building is a wonder to behold. It is hard to take in all the visually stunning elements, from Henry Moore's travertine marble altar, carved in 1972, to the surrounding brightly coloured abstract kneelers designed by Patrick Heron. The church is also famous for having Dr Chad Vara, founder of the Samaritans, as its rector for over fifty years. The original telephone used by people contacting the befriending service can be seen to the right of the main door.

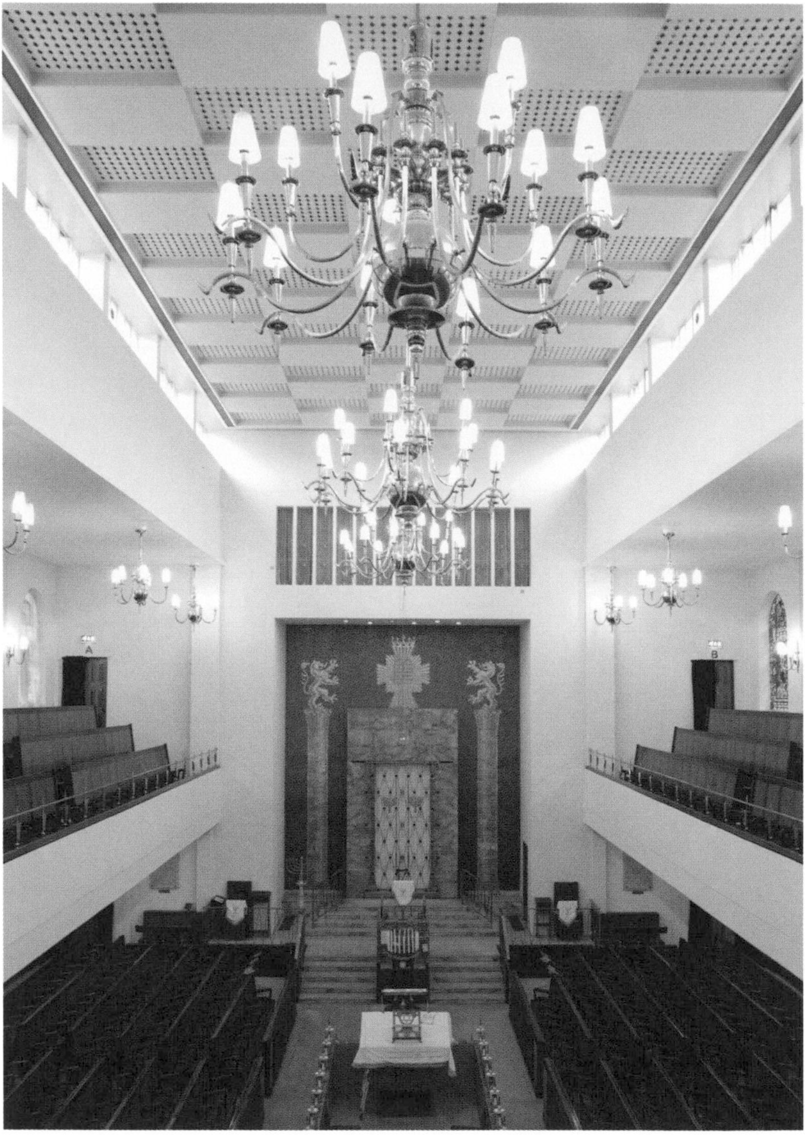

The Central Synagogue

36–40 Hallam Street, W1W 6NW ☎ 020 7580 1355
Free www.centralsynagogue.org.uk
Open Monday–Thursday 9am–3.30pm, services 7.40am and 1.15pm, and on Friday evening and Saturday
Tube Oxford Circus, Warren Street, Great Portland Street, Regent's Park
Bus 18, 27, 30, 88, 205, 453, C2
The synagogue is wheelchair accessible – ring in advance to arrange access. There is a loop for people with hearing loss

Heavily bombed in the Second World War, the original nineteenth-century edifice was replaced by this 1950s building. The main Orthodox synagogue in central London, its interior is a good example of postwar architecture and design. The carved wooden doors have attractive stylised semi-abstract reliefs, and the polished brass finials look good against the mustard-yellow carpet and coral marble. Remains of the prewar synagogue were found recently, including antique prints of the interior which now hang on the walls near the entrance. This is a very quiet, peaceful space to visit during the week.

Grosvenor Chapel

24 South Audley Street, W1K 2PA ☎ 020 7499 1684 **Free** www.grosvenorchapel.org.uk
Open Daily 9am–4pm, daily prayer weekdays 12.30pm
Tube Green Park, Hyde Park Corner **Bus** 2, 10, 16, 36, 73, 82, 84, 137, 148, 414, 436
The chapel has a portable ramp which it can lay over the front entrance steps if
notified in advance and there is also access to an adapted toilet

This gracious small church has been here since 1730 and, although it is located in
upmarket Mayfair, the congregation now comes from all over London. The building is
a simple classical form of an unadorned rectangular box with arched windows in the
side walls. The box pews were removed many years ago, but otherwise the interior is
largely intact. A few notable Londoners are buried here, including Lady Mary Wortley
Montagu, who introduced smallpox inoculation to England in 1718. Other famous
members of the congregation were Florence Nightingale and the Poet Laureate Sir
John Betjeman. The chapel is renowned for its music, and free lunchtime concerts
are held here throughout the year.

St Mary's Rotherhithe

St Marychurch Street, SE16 4JE
☎ 020 7394 3394
Free www.stmaryrotherhithe.org
Open by appointment **Tube** Canada
Water, Bermondsey **Train** Rotherhithe
Bus 1, 47, 188, 381, C10
The church is not wheelchair accessible

Captain Christopher Jones, Master of
the ship *The Mayflower*, set off for the
New World with pilgrims from this
Rotherhithe church. It was built in 1715
but remodelled by William Butterworth
in the nineteenth century, with marble
steps and a beautiful altar.

St Olave's

Hart Street, EC3R 7NB ☎ 020 7488 4318
Free www.sanctuaryinthecity.net/
St-Olaves.html **Open** Weekdays 9am–
5pm, closed after Christmas and Easter
and in August **Tube** Monument **Train**
Fenchurch Street **Bus** 15, 40
The church is wheelchair accessible

One of the few medieval buildings to
survive the Great Fire of London, St
Olave's has the tranquil atmosphere
of a country parish church. The diarist
Samuel Pepys lived in the parish for 14
years from 1660 and is buried here, in
what he called 'our own church'.

St George's Hanover Square

2a Mill Street, W1S 1FX ☎ 020 7629 0874 **Free** www.stgeorgeshanoversquare.org
Open Monday–Friday 8am–4pm, Wednesday to 6pm, Sunday services 8am to midday,
closed Bank Holidays
Tube Oxford Circus **Bus** 6, 10, 23, 55, 73, 88, 98, 139, 159, 453, C2
Ring in advance to request the ramp for wheelchair access. There is no accessible
toilet in the church

This handsome eighteenth-century church is open for private prayer and quiet visits
during the day, and it is a very calm place to find some respite from the crowds in
nearby Oxford Street. The interior hasn't changed much in the last three hundred
years, and the dark wooden pews and simple interior make this a restful place.
George Frideric Handel was an active parishioner and had a pew in the church, which
was built just after he came to live in the area in 1724. With its gold and white painted
ceiling, Doric pillars and brass chandeliers, the church is the perfect setting for
concerts by the European Union Baroque Orchestra and other musicians.

St Paul's Knightsbridge

32a Wilton Place, SW1X 8SH ☎ 020 7201 9999
Free www.stpaulsknightsbridge.org
Open Daily 9am–6pm, guided silent meditation Tuesday 7.30am
Tube Hyde Park Corner, Knightsbridge **Bus** 9, 10, 14, 19, 22, 52, 74, 137, 434
The church is wheelchair accessible

This large, visually stunning church was consecrated in 1863, and was immediately popular, with a large congregation turning up each Sunday morning. The richly decorated church was the first in London to support the Oxford Movement and its ornate design reflects the Anglo-Catholic ideals of the day. The church has an ambulatory, a spacious walkway around the outside of the nave, where the *via dolorosa* – the stages of Jesus carrying the cross – are depicted on cream and terracotta wall tiles. The nineteenth-century font carved with biblical scenes near the back of the church is especially beautiful.

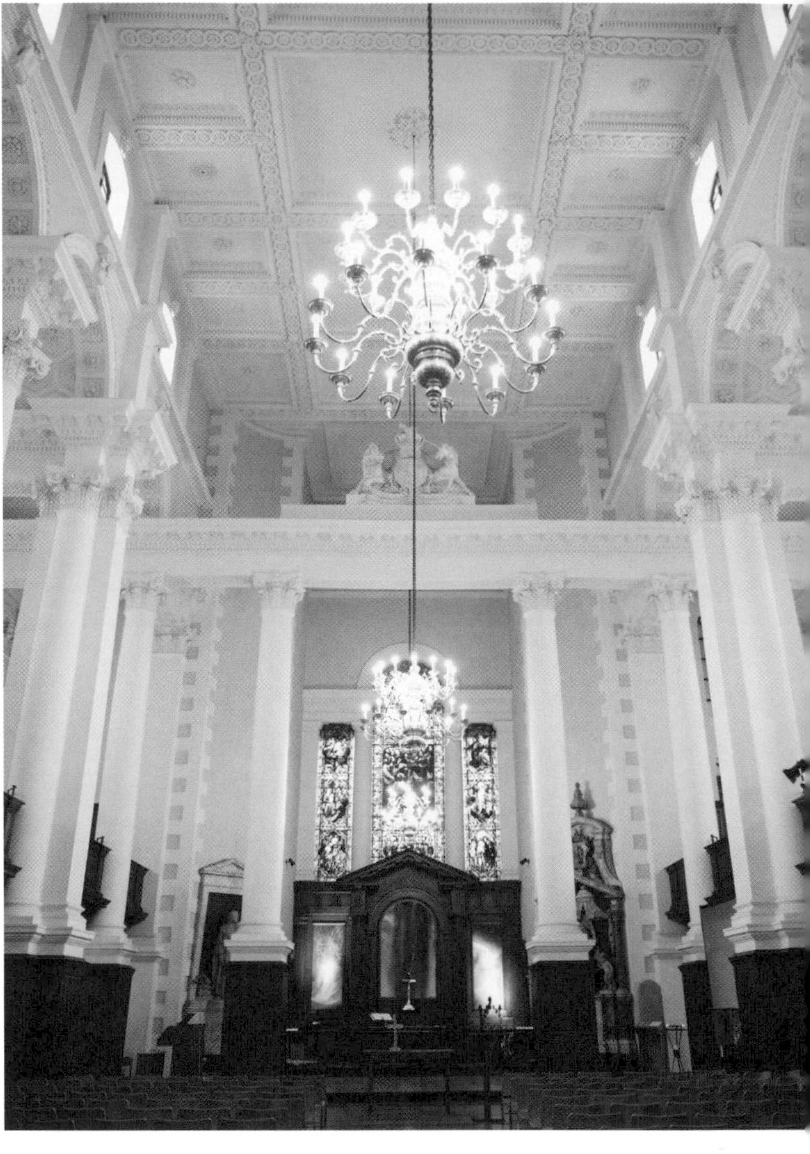

Christ Church Spitalfields

Commercial Street, E1 6LY ☎ 020 7377 6793
Free www.ccspitalfields.org
Open Weekdays 10am–4pm, daily prayer 9am, Sunday 1–4pm, service Tuesday 1.15pm, Lunchtime recital 1st Friday of the month 1.10–2pm
Tube Liverpool Street, Aldgate East **Train** Shoreditch High Street
Bus 25, 67, 78, 205, 254
The church is wheelchair accessible

This outstanding Nicholas Hawksmoor church took fifteen years to build and was eventually completed in 1729. Many French Huguenot silk weavers living nearby were practising as Nonconformists at a time when the Fifty New Churches Act of 1711 was passed. Four commissions oversaw the erection of twelve new churches in London, one of which is Hawksmoor's Spitalfields masterpiece. The magnificent Richard Bridge organ arrived a few years later in 1735 and has survived since the age of Handel. After the church fell into disrepair in the twentieth century, it took 25 years to restore, and now has a beautiful oak and white-painted interior. The building is now used as much as a performance space as a place of worship, and hosts the Spitalfields Festival and other events.

Places near water

Shadwell Basin
3–4 Shadwell Pierhead, Glamis Road, London E1W 3TD ☎ 020 7481 4210
Free www.shadwell-basin.co.uk
Open All day and night, seven days a week
DLR Shadwell, Limehouse **Bus** 15, 100, 115, 135, D3
The paths are wheelchair accessible

On a sunny autumn Sunday morning, only a couple of people could be seen walking around the tranquil Shadwell Basin. This peaceful man-made port has canal boats and other floating craft and perhaps only locals and boat owners know of its existence. Walking along the brick-lined waterfront, the vistas constantly change, making this an interesting place to go for a stroll. Fishing is also permitted during daylight hours, although not many people seem to take up this very quiet activity. With St Paul's Shadwell's spire in the distance, this calm place feels almost rural.

The Regent's Canal at Broadway Market

Regent's Row, Hackney E8 4PH ☎ Canal River Trust 0303 040 4040
Free www.canalrivertrust.org.uk/canals-and-rivers/regents-canal,
www.broadwaymarket.co.uk
Open All day every day, but safer during daytime than after dark
Tube Cambridge Heath, London Fields **Train** Haggerston **Bus** 236, 394
There is a wheelchair accessible path by the bridge

The Regent's Canal wends its way through many different parts of London, including this increasingly trendy part of Hackney. A Site of Metropolitan Importance for Nature Conservation, the waterway is an area of natural biodiversity and a much more tranquil place to walk or cycle than at street level. Named one of the top ten street markets in London, Broadway Market round the corner is a good place to pick up a rye loaf and soft goats' cheese for a spontaneous picnic by the water. Walk further on and you will find the stark remains of an empty gasometer, an idyllic sight for anyone who feels at all romantic about industrial landscapes.

East India Dock Basin

Orchard Place, E14 9QS ☎ 08456 770 600
Free www.visitleevalley.org.uk/en/content/cms/nature/nature-reserve/bow-creek,
www.wildlondon.org.uk
Open All day every day
DLR East India **Bus** 277
East India Dock Basin is wheelchair accessible

One of the most tranquil places in East London, this former dock used to receive shipments from all over the world. Instead of the shouts of dockers unloading heavy sacks of spices from sailing clippers, nowadays you will mainly hear birds landing on the water. Now a nature reserve, the East India Dock is managed by the London Wildlife Trust and contains the only saltmarsh in this area. This is an important centre for nesting wildlife, from arctic terns to snipe, sandmartins, kingfishers and grey herons. The Thames Path runs along the edge of the basin, so you can walk beside the water, keeping an eye out for burnet companion moths and long-tailed blue butterflies.

Dulwich Park

College Road, Dulwich SE21 7BQ ☎ 020 7525 2000
Free www.southwark.gov.uk/info/461/a_to_z_of_parks/1296/dulwich_park/1,
www.dulwichgoinggreener.org.uk/dulwich-vegetable-garden
Open Daily 7.30am–dusk, café Monday–Friday 8.30am–5.30pm, weekend 9am–5.30pm
Train West Dulwich, North Dulwich, Forest Hill **Bus** P4, P13
The park has excellent, wide paths and wheelchair accessible toilets

This 29-hectare Green Flag Award-winning park has a large boating lake, a simple
but stylish wooden walkway over streams and a variety of wildfowl that appreciate the
imaginative reed planting. The café plays music, sadly, but the outdoor tables can be
very pleasant places to enjoy a salad lunch or a pot of tea and cake. The gardeners
have developed a drought-resistant garden that shows the wide range of plants that
can be grown with little water. And if you like your flora to be edible, the vegetable
garden behind the Rosebery Lodge is full of very healthy-looking chard, leeks and
purple carrots grown by local enthusiasts. There are bicycles for hire in the park and
guided walks on Wednesday mornings.

Kyoto Garden, Holland Park

Ilchester Place, W8 6LU, entrances on Campden Hill and Abbotsbury Road
☎ 020 7602 2226 **Free**
www.rbkc.gov.uk/leisureandlibraries/parksandgardens/yourlocalpark/hollandpark
Open Daily 7.30am–30 minutes before dusk
Tube Holland Park, Kensington Olympia, High Street Kensington
Bus 9, 10, 27, 74, 94, 148, 295, 316, 328, C1, C3
Most of the paths are wheelchair accessible but rather uneven. Enter by the path to
the left of the main steps

A gift from the Japanese for British support after the Kyoto earthquake of the mid-
1990s, this entrancing garden is one of the most beautiful corners of London. Nearly
everything is in miniature, from bright pink azaleas to exquisite pine trees. Dark grey,
wrinkled rocks surround a pretty waterfall which descends into a still pond, where
golden carp swim among the shadows. In autumn the leaves of the 'Red Dragon'
Japanese maples turn bright red, while in spring the magnolia petals transform the
garden into a pink and white paradise. Intended for calm contemplation, this is a
restful place to wander among silver birch and Mexican orange blossom.

Deptford Creek

Creekside, Deptford SE8 4SA, path to
the left of the ornate metal gates at
Creekside Discovery Centre (CDC)
☎ 020 8692 9922 CDC **Free** but there is
a fee for the low-tide walk at CDC
www.creeksidecentre.org.uk/events/
low-tide-walks **Open** All day every day
DLR Deptford Bridge, Greenwich
Bus 47, 53, 177
The paths are accessible, except for
wading through the mudflats

At dusk the fading light accentuates the
stark outlines of the industrial relics
above the old brick arches. The mudflat
wading tours follow the river at low tide.

The Regent's Canal at Wharf Road

Entrances on Danbury Street and Wharf
Road, N1 8PZ ☎ 020 7387 5333
Free www.canalrivertrust.org.uk,
www.friendsofregentscanal.org
Information at The Lock Keeper's
Cottage, 289 Camden High St, NW1 7BX
Open All day every day
Tube Old Street **Bus** 43, 205, 214, 394
Wheelchair access from Danbury Street
Bridge

Completed in 1820, this waterway,
surrounded by lime and willow trees,
is now a tranquil place to watch boats
pass by.

Emirates Airline Cable Cars

Ticket points at North Greenwich Tube or Royal Victoria DLR
☎ TFL travel information line 0843 222 1234
£ www.tfl.gov.uk/gettingaround/23850.aspx, www.emiratesairline.co.uk
Open 28 March–30 September Monday–Friday 7am–9pm, Saturday 8am–9pm,
Sunday 9am–9pm, 1 October–27 March closes 1 hour earlier
Tube North Greenwich **DLR** Royal Victoria **Bus** 108, 188, 474
There is wheelchair access to the cable cars and accessible toilets in the café by the
ticket office at North Greenwich

Over 3 million journeys have been made on the Emirates Airline but it doesn't feel
crowded once you are inside your own small cubicle. This is a rather futuristic way
to glide very quietly across East London. The gently moving cable cars allow you to
appreciate views of the River Thames from high in the sky. Sitting in your glass pod,
all you can hear is your own breathing and the soft pulling of cables as the cars
ascend and descend. The airline may not run if there is a threat of storms or high
winds, so if the weather looks dramatic you can instead walk along the Thames Path.

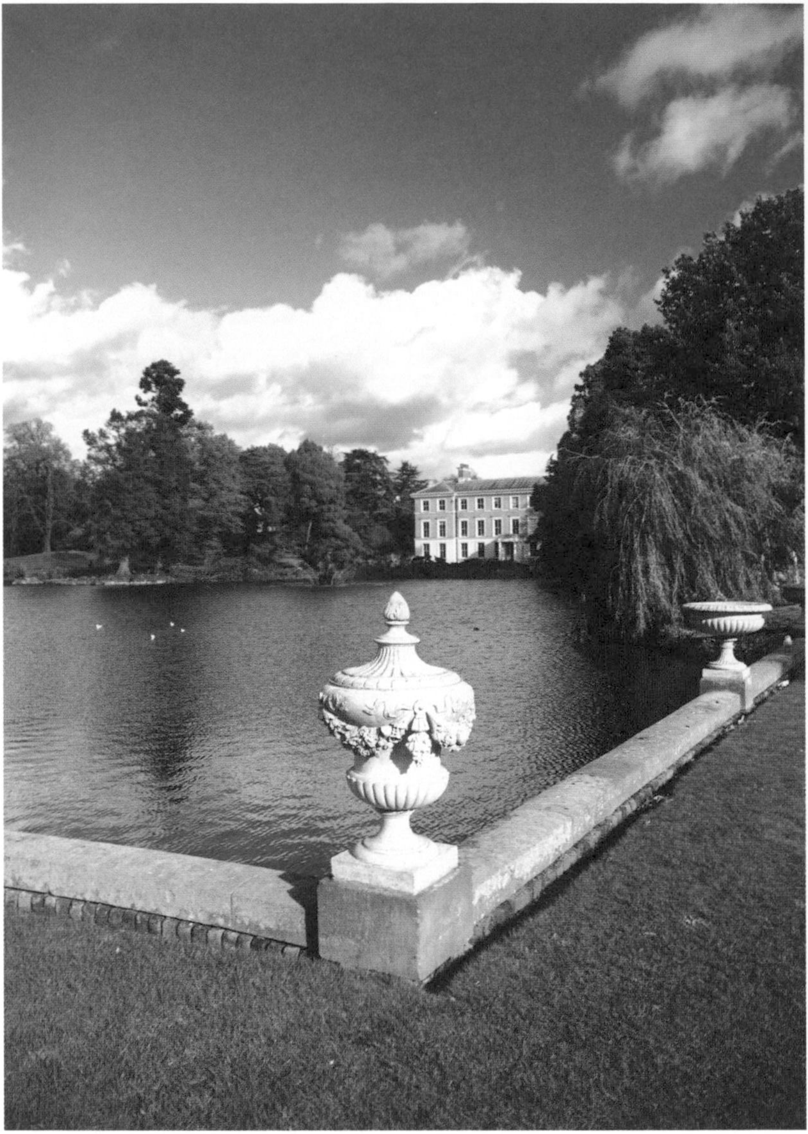

Kew Gardens

Royal Botanic Gardens, Kew, Richmond TW9 3AB ☎ 020 8332 5655
£ www.kew.org
Open Daily 9.30am–around 4.15pm winter, 6pm summer
Tube Kew Gardens **Train** Kew Bridge **Bus** 65, 237, 267, 391
The gardens, glasshouses and cafés are wheelchair accessible

Although Kew Gardens can get busy, it is capacious enough to give the impression that you are walking round a tranquil landscape, furnished with lakes, exotic plants and small bowers. One of the quietest corners is the exquisite Marianne North Gallery, which first opened in 1882 and is one of the few permanent solo exhibitions by a female artist in Britain. Other exhibitions in Kew Gardens include displays of botanical illustrations, garden photography and other artwork inspired by the natural world. If you prefer nature to be live rather than drawn, the lake by the main entrance is a very peaceful place to watch birds arrive and depart, even in the frosty winter months.

Places to sit

Porchester Square

Porchester Road, W2 6AW
Free www.westminster.gov.uk/porchester-square-garden
Open Daily 8am–dusk
Tube Royal Oak **Bus** 7, 18, 23, 36
The gardens are wheelchair accessible

At one end of these formal gardens is the much-revered Porchester Hall, where concerts and literary events are held throughout the year. This impressive carved Portland stone building is almost completely hidden in summer, however, as tall London plane and Indian horse chestnut trees surround the green lawns and variegated tulip displays. Despite the clamour of busy shopping streets nearby, this is a very restful place to sit and browse the paper or chat about gentle things with a friend. Porchester Hall also has a public library, so London residents can borrow a few books then sit on one of the park benches to read, surrounded by cherry blossom in spring.

Hanover Square Gardens
Hanover Square, W1F 5JF
Free www.westminster.gov.uk/hanover-square-garden
Open Monday–Saturday 8am–dusk, Sunday 9am–dusk
Tube Oxford Circus **Bus** 3, 6, 7, 8, 10, 12, 13, 15, 23, 25, 55, 73, 88, 94, 98,
139, 159, 176, 390, 453, C2
Hanover Square is wheelchair accessible

Named in honour of King George I, the Elector of Hanover in Germany, Hanover
Square Gardens were first laid out in 1717. No longer overlooked by an eighteenth-
century workhouse crammed with 700 people, this Mayfair square is now home to
squirrels, birds and anyone who wants to find some respite from the commercial
excesses of nearby Oxford Street. Although it is surrounded by London streets, the
sound of cars is masked by tall trees and luxuriant hedges. An 1831 monument to
William Pitt the Younger, one of England's most admired prime ministers, is on the
south side of the square but is often overlooked by people sitting on the benches.

Westbourne Gardens

Westbourne Gardens, Royal Oak, W2
☎ Westminster City Council Built Environment 020 7641 2513
Free www.westminster.gov.uk/parks-gardens-and-open-spaces
Open Monday–Sunday 8am–dusk
Tube Royal Oak **Bus** 18, 27, 36, 70
The gardens are wheelchair accessible

One of a few green spaces within the Bayswater conservation area, Westbourne Gardens is surrounded by handsome, white stucco nineteenth-century terraced houses. This feels like a civilised place to appreciate London from a less frenetic vantage point. This small West London garden with its large fig tree and pink chrysanthemums offers welcome respite from the busy roads and shopping streets nearby. This is the perfect place to sit and read or just look up at the trees. You don't have to be a wealthy homeowner living in one of the surrounding properties – anyone can walk here and find a seat on the hexagonal park bench.

Dalston Eastern Curve Garden

13 Dalston Lane, Hackney E8 3DF
Free www.dalstongarden.org
Open Daily 11am–dusk, café 11am–7pm
and later for evening events
Train Dalston Junction, Dalston
Kingsland **Bus** 30, 38, 76, 149, 236, 242,
243, 277, 488
The garden is wheelchair accessible

Local people come here to sit and
appreciate the flowers, to chat with their
friends or to tend their speckled green
courgettes and climbing beans. Behind
an inviting arbour you can find herbs
growing in beds made of recycled wood.
You can also have tea and cake at the
lovely café near the entrance.

Elder Street Garden

Entrances on Lamb Street and Spital
Square, E1 6UJ **Free**
Open Monday–Friday 8am–dusk
Tube Liverpool Street **Train** Shoreditch
High Street **Bus** 8, 26, 35, 42, 47, 48, 78,
135, 149, 342, 344, 388
The gardens are wheelchair accessible

These private gardens can be found at
the northern end of Spitalfields Market.
Sit around two rectangular lawns
surrounded by herbaceous borders.
The foliage is mainly glossy-leaved
evergreens except for a few delicate
silver birch trees on a small hill.

Harleyford Road Community Gardens

Entrances on 37 Bonnington Square or Harleyford Road, SW8 1TF
Free www.ovalpartnership.org.uk/kennington-oval-vauxhall-history/parks-and-green-spaces/harleyford-road-community-gardens.html
Open Daily 10am–sunset
Tube Vauxhall, Oval **Bus** 2, 36, 88, 185, 436
The gardens are mostly wheelchair accessible as are the toilets

In the mid-1980s local residents began to grow vegetables on what was a neglected 1.5-acre wasteland, sowing the seeds for what is now a flourishing community garden, still maintained by local people. With only a few trees to work with, they planted many bushes and flowers, created wooden walkways and dug a tranquil pond. Mosaic paths in this secret wildlife garden lead to a children's play area at one end, and there is a picnic table for anyone to use whenever the weather is clement.

Quaker Gardens

Bunhill Fields Meeting House, Quaker Court, Banner Street, EC1Y 8QQ
☎ 07724 426 316
Free www.quaker.org.uk/bunhill-fields, www.studymore.org.uk/bunhill.htm
Open All day every day, Kadampa Buddhist meditation in Meeting House Monday 7pm, Quaker meeting for worship Sunday 11am
Tube Old Street **Bus** 21, 43, 55, 76, 135, 141, 205, 214, 243, 271
The gardens are wheelchair accessible

The huge London plane tree in the centre of this garden stands like an immense giant above the benches and paths. Now the garden for the Meeting House, this historic Quaker burial ground is where George Fox, one of the founders of Quakerism, is interred. Most of the Quaker buildings here were destroyed during the Second World War, but the former caretaker's cottage remains and is where meeting for worship now takes place on Sunday. Beneath the leafy canopy, this is a secluded place to sit quietly outdoors. If you prefer to sit in silence with other people, you can also join the weekly gathering in the Meeting House.

St Luke's Church Gardens

161 Old Street, EC1V 9NG ☎ 020 7527 2000
Free www.islington.gov.uk/services/parks-environment/parks/your_parks/
greenspace_az/greenspace_st/Pages/st_lukes.aspx
Open Daily 8am–dusk
Tube Old Street **Bus** 4, 55, 243, 812
There are accessible entrances on Helmet Row and St Luke's Close

This handsome eighteenth-century Hawksmoor church is now the home of the
London Symphony Orchestra, and many performances take place in this music
education centre. Behind the church, the lawns are peaceful places to walk or sit and
read on one of the wooden benches. In summer the flower beds are full of roses, and
birds congregate around the hanging feeders. This garden has been a public space
since the 1870s, and is now an important site for urban wildlife which thrives among
the yellow-flowering berberis and coral japonica shrubs. At the northern end you can
also relax in Ironmonger Row Leisure Centre and their Spa London Turkish Baths.

Lambeth High Street Recreation Ground
off Lambeth Walk, SE11, entrances on corner of Old Paradise Street,
Lambeth High Street and Whitgift Street **Free**
Open All day every day
Tube Vauxhall, Lambeth North **Bus** 3, 77, 344, 360
The garden is wheelchair accessible

This is a small garden with raised hillocks and mature copper beech trees, well hidden behind low-rise, postwar housing. It is a nice short cut through to Lambeth Walk from the River Thames, close to Beaconsfield Art Café and nearby Gasworks. Up to now the area has not been much visited, but this will change with the opening of the new Damien Hirst gallery in nearby Newport Street. After wending your way through the crowds at this new contemporary art space, walk round the corner to find this secret garden. At dusk you might see urban foxes snuffling along the paths and, for a few short days in early May, Old Paradise Street is full of cherry blossom.

Bethnal Green Gardens

Cambridge Heath Road, E2 0HL ☎ 020 7364 3348
Free www.towerhamlets.gov.uk/lgsl/451-500/461_parks/bethnal_green_gardens.aspx
Open Daily dawn–dusk
Tube Bethnal Green **Bus** 8, 106, 205, 253, 254, 309, 388, D3, D6
The gardens are wheelchair accessible

With a library at one end and the Museum of Childhood at the other, this East End
park has some culturally enlightened neighbours. Perhaps because of the way
the trees were laid out at spacious intervals in the nineteenth century, sitting in
these gardens feels like being in a relaxed outdoor living room. There are squirrels
running along fences, elderflowers blossoming in the summer and rather raucous
ring-necked parakeets flying between the branches of London plane trees. After
sitting for a while, pay a visit to the Herald Street art galleries nearby, or do your own
sketch in the Bethnal Green outdoor life drawing class, held on Saturdays (see the
poster at St John's Church, Roman Road for details).

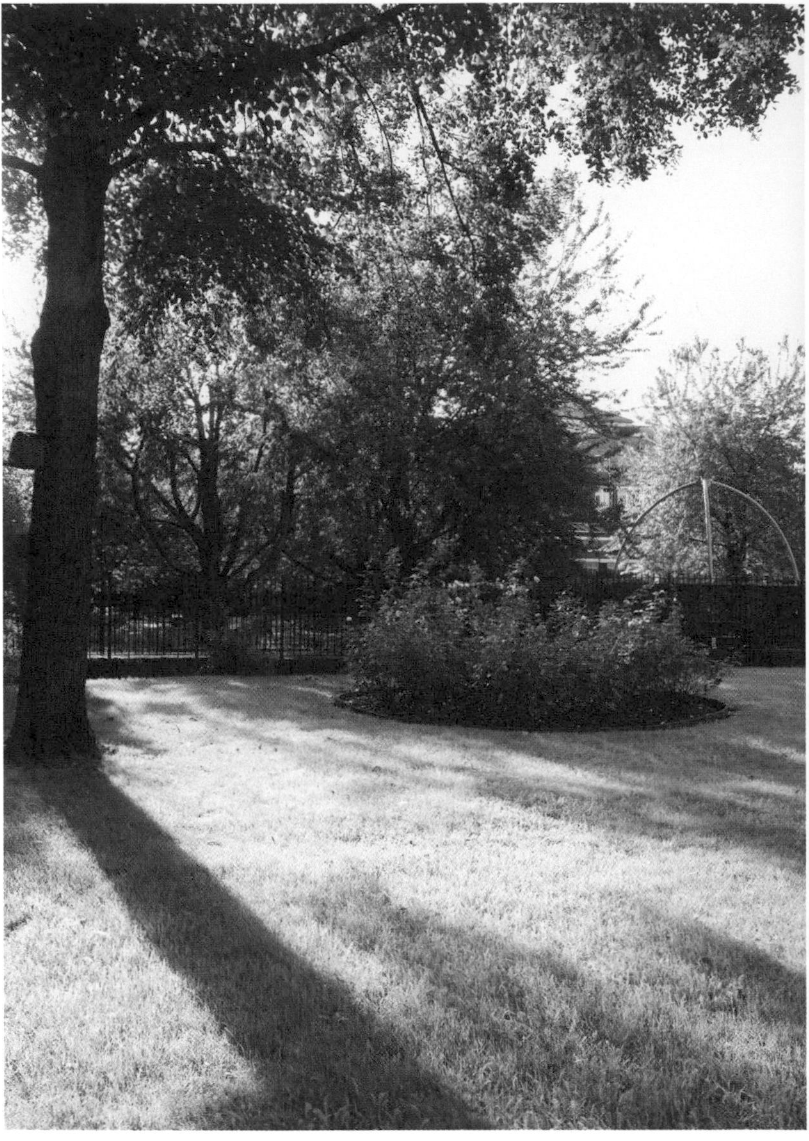

Radnor Street Gardens

Entrances on corner of Radnor Street and Lizard Street, off City Road, EC1

☎ 020 7527 2000

Free www.islington.gov.uk/services/parks-environment/parks/your_parks/greenspace_az/greenspace_r/Pages/radnor_street.aspx

Open Daily 8am–dusk

Tube Old Street **Bus** 43, 205, 215

The gardens are wheelchair accessible

The area around Old Street has been nicknamed Silicon Roundabout, due to the high number of IT companies who have offices or workstations here. Sitting facing computer screens all day, many workers will be unaware that there are some attractive small gardens a few minutes' walk away. Walking through this small garden will probably help anyone feel refreshed and able to concentrate better. Large round rocks act as giant stepping stones for younger digital experts to play on while grown-ups will appreciate sitting nearby on a long granite bench beneath shady cherry trees.

Calthorpe Gardens

258–74 Grays Inn Road, WC1X 8LH ☎ 0207 837 8019
Free www.calthorpeproject.org.uk
Open Monday–Friday 10am–6pm summer, 9am–5pm winter, Saturday and Sunday
12–6pm all year, see website for class timetables
Tube King's Cross, Chancery Lane **Bus** 17, 45, 46
The garden is wheelchair accessible

This spacious inner-city green oasis is much more than just an attractive garden
with a beehive, it's also a community project which involves local people in exciting
horticultural projects. A revolutionary new composting system called anaerobic
digestion has been installed in the greenhouse and will show gardeners how to
transform their waste into renewable energy. If you don't have your own vegetable
plot, come and see the edible things growing here and take a stroll around the wild
garden planted with native species. In fact, you won't have much time to sit down,
as there are so many interesting things to do. You can join a Pilates class, learn
Kundalini yoga or practise gong meditation in the beautifully designed community
room.

Boundary Gardens
Arnold Circus, E2 7JS ☎ 07903 397 431
Free www.foac.org.uk
Open All day every day
Train Shoreditch High Street **Bus** 26, 35, 47, 48, 55, 149, 242, 243
The gardens are not wheelchair accessible

Boundary Gardens are not that well known, except by people who live in the vicinity.
Covering a huge mound, this leafy open space has a bandstand at the top and many
benches surrounding the circular knoll. Friends often meet here, enjoying each
other's company while sitting among the trees. The hillock was built with rubble
from the demolished Old Nichol slum and has impressive views of the nearby Grade
II-listed Boundary Estate, an early terracotta brick housing development opened by
the Prince of Wales in 1900, described by some as the world's first council housing.

Millbank Gardens
John Islip Street, SW1P 4RG, entrance also on Herrick Street
Free www.westminster.gov.uk/parks-gardens-and-open-spaces
Open Daily 8am–dusk
Tube Victoria, Vauxhall **Bus** 88, C10
The gardens are wheelchair accessible

Located directly behind Tate Britain, this is a good place to sit and appreciate the outdoors after a visit to an exhibition. Although it is not the most spectacular garden in the city, it is simply laid out and tidy with small grass lawns that offer a softer side to the city. It is usually less crowded than the stone plazas outside the Tate. The pollarded maples in the street surrounding the gardens are like dramatic sculptures with their strange protuberances, while inside you can find lush bamboo bushes, and a few rowan and holly trees that produce pretty red berries in autumn.

St George's Gardens
Bloomsbury WC1, entrances on Handel Street and Heathcote Street ☎ 020 7974 1693
Free www.friendsofstgeorgesgardens.org.uk
Open Daily, during daylight hours
Tube Russell Square, King's Cross **Bus** 17, 45, 46
The gardens are wheelchair accessible and include a sensory garden for people with impaired sight

A public garden was created from the old burial ground of St George's Church as early as 1884 and the cemetery of St George the Martyr was added a few years later, after some initial opposition. Despite the gardens having been here for over 130 years, few people know of their existence. Hidden behind a former philanthropic orphanage, now the Foundling Museum, the gardens still have a number of old, ivy-clad tombstones among the grass lawns. Notorious for being the first site where a grave robber stole a body for medical dissection in 1777, nowadays the gardens are among the most tranquil green spaces in central London.

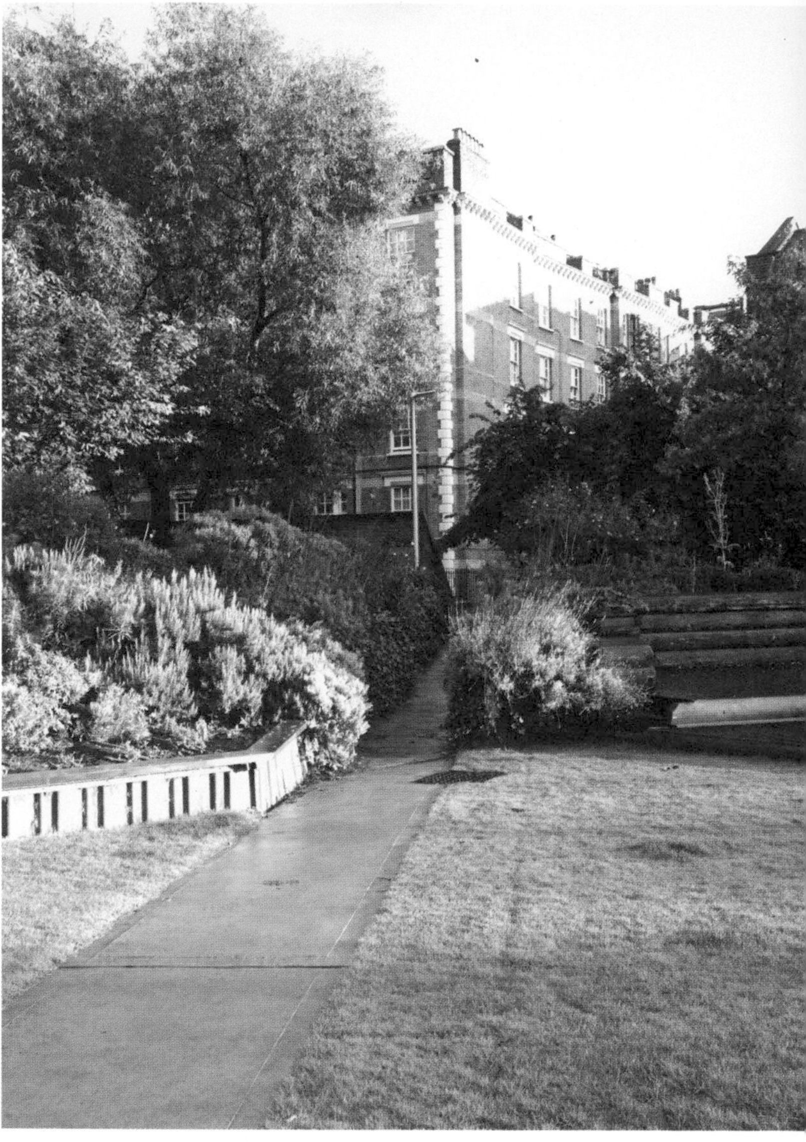

Mint Street Park

Mint Street, SE1, entrances on Caleb Street and Southwark Bridge Road
☎ 020 7525 2000 **Free**
www.southwark.gov.uk/info/461/a_to_z_of_parks/657/smaller_parks_and_gardens/1
Open All day every day
Tube Borough **Bus** 344
The park is wheelchair accessible

This Bermondsey Park has been beautifully re-designed and now has some judicious planting in the herbaceous borders. The site of the former Evelina Children's Hospital, it is now a welcome open space in a built-up area. There are sloped areas, ideal for lying down to sunbathe on sunny days, and a small outdoor gym for when you are feeling fit. Surrounded by nineteenth-century apartments, this medium-sized park offers welcome respite for local people. Just before sunset, the rockeries turn golden in the evening light, making this an idyllic place for a stroll after work.

The Walks, Gray's Inn Gardens

4 Gray's Inn Square, WC1R 5DX, entrances on corner of Jockey's Fields and
Sandland Street ☎ 0207 458 7800
Free www.graysinn.info
Open Monday–Friday 12–2.30pm, surrounding paths 8am–8pm
Tube Chancery Lane, Holborn **Bus** 8, 19, 25, 38, 45, 55, 242, 341, 521
There is wheelchair access to the paths around the Walks, but there is gravel at the
entrance

Gray's Inn is the smallest of the Law Courts in London, but this is hard to tell from the
expanse of gracious terraced buildings surrounding these tranquil lawns. Law clerks
and their apprentices have been working on the present site since the late fourteenth
century, and barristers and solicitors still obtain their vocational qualifications and
legal experience in these eminent rooms. Known as the Walks, the gardens were laid
out by Sir Francis Bacon during his time as Treasurer here in 1606. Charles Dickens
was an articled clerk in one of the adjacent solicitors' offices, making this the ideal
place to sit on a bench reading *Bleak House*.

Portsoken Street Garden
Corner of Portsoken Street and Goodman Yard, E1 8BN
☎ 020 7332 3503 **Free**
www.cityoflondon.gov.uk/things-to-do/green-spaces/city-gardens/Documents/Tree-trail-City-of-London.pdf
Open Monday–Friday 8am–7pm or dusk, whichever is earlier
Tube Tower Hill **DLR** Tower Gateway **Bus** 42, 78, 100, 551
The garden is wheelchair accessible

The first thing that catches your eye in Portsoken Street Garden is the unusual living wall made of numerous plants growing on the side of a modern, north-facing building. The lush greenery provides a dramatic backdrop to this small garden near Tower Hill. The wildlife pond is surrounded by tall grasses and thick-stemmed reeds, while pink onion flowers border the small lawns. This may not be the Hanging Gardens of Babylon, but for a quick break at lunchtime it is a nice alternative to sitting at your desk trying not to look at the computer screen.

St Dunstan in the East

St Dunstan's Hill, off Lower Thames Street, EC3R 8DX
Free www.cityoflondon.gov.uk/things-to-do/green-spaces/city-gardens/visitor-
information/Pages/St-Dunstan-in-the-East.aspx
Open Daily 8am–7pm or dusk, whichever is earlier
Tube Monument, Tower Hill **Bus** 15, 42, 78, 100, RV1
St Dunstan in the East has an accessible entrance in Idol Lane

After St Dunstan's was bombed in the 1940s, the ruins of Christopher Wren's
eighteenth-century church were turned into a pretty, sheltered garden on the edge
of the City of London. Wooden benches surround a circular cobbled pattern on the
ground, providing a focus at the centre of one of the secluded areas, while trailing
vines and spiky-leaved exotic plants look stunning by the entrance. Keep an eye out
for the large old fig tree which survived the attacks – a plaque explains its history,
just behind where it still grows today.

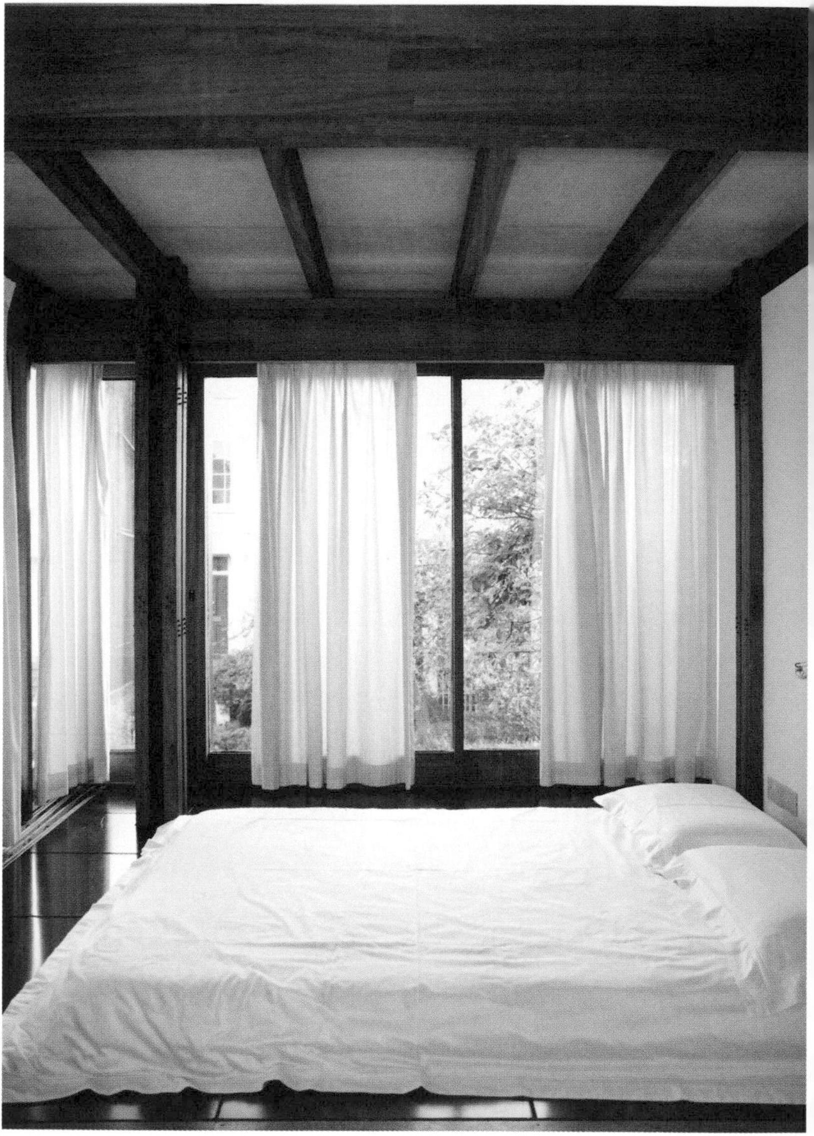

Places to stay

66 Camden Square B&B
66 Camden Square, NW1 9XD ☎ 020 7485 4622
Tube Camden Town, Kentish Town **Train** Camden Road
Bus 29, 134, 214, 253, 390, 393
The house is not wheelchair accessible

This beautiful wooden-framed house was designed by the architect owner, whose impeccable taste also extends to the simple, white-walled, Japanese-inspired guest bedroom. The only sound you will hear in this light-filled house might be the occasional squawk of Peckham, the blue and gold macaw, who lives downstairs. It is a real surprise to find somewhere as lovely and peaceful within walking distance of Camden Tube. After enjoying all the noisy delights of Camden Market at the weekend, this is the perfect place to bed down for the night.

B&B Belgravia

64–66 Ebury Street, SW1W 9QD ☎ 020 7259 8570
www.bb-belgravia.com
Tube Sloane Square, Victoria **Bus** 2, 11, 24, 148, 170, 211, 507, 702, C1, C10
There is one wheelchair accessible room

This handsome Grade II-listed terraced building in genteel Belgravia was converted
into a boutique hotel in 2004, and two interconnected buildings now provide
comfortable accommodation in the heart of the city. The quiet guest lounge is open
during the day for guests to help themselves to coffee and Earl Grey and green teas.
The rooms are compact, so if you want to read downstairs a small selection of novels
can be found on the open shelves for anyone to borrow. With its grey slate stones
and wooden furniture, the small garden at the rear feels simple and uncluttered. The
hotel also lends out bicycles to guests – one of the quietest ways to get round London.

Putney Bed & Breakfast

11 Lytton Grove, SW15 2EP ☎ 0208 780 1255
www.putneybedandbreakfast.com
Tube East Putney **Train** Putney **Bus** 14, 22, 85, 93
The house is not wheelchair accessible

Former guests describe this welcoming bed and breakfast as 'a little taste of
traditional England' and it is easy to see why. The welcoming owner makes her own
apple, pear and vanilla compôte for breakfast, and uses whatever fruit is in season to
create luscious preserves. With the largest garden in Putney, this is one of the most
rural locations in the vicinity. The rear bedroom overlooks hornbeams, sycamores,
oaks and climbing roses and you will probably be gently woken by birdsong in the
morning. The house was built in the 1920s by a junior member of the Cartier family
and President de Gaulle once had dinner here, a bit too early in the twentieth century
to appreciate the current owner's delicious home-made raspberry jam.

Forest Lodge

Drax Avenue, SW20 0EY
☎ 020 8946 3253 www.
thewimbledonbedandbreakfast.com
Tube and **Train** Raynes Park,
Wimbledon **Bus** 57, 200
The bedrooms are inaccessible to
wheelchair users

This spacious 1920s house feels like a
home from home. Located in a tranquil
road, this is one of the most rural places
to stay in London. The immaculate
upstairs bedrooms are incredibly quiet:
all you will hear at night is the rustle of
leaves in the trees.

John and Norma's Homestay B&B

74 Coniston Road, Muswell Hill N10 2BN
☎ 020 8444 8127 www.74coniston.com
Tube Bounds Green
Bus 43, 102, 134, 144, 221, 234, 299
Not wheelchair accessible

Wake up to birdsong in this lovely large
Victorian house in Muswell Hill. With
views towards Alexandra Park, this is
an exceptionally quiet place to stay. You
might see migrating geese overhead or
blue tits in the garden. John and Norma
met at art school and are generous
hosts who offer guests a warm welcome
and lavish vegetarian breakfasts.

Fox Hill B&B

24 Fox Hill, Crystal Palace SE19 2XE ☎ 020 8768 0059
www.foxhill-bandb.co.uk
Train Crystal Palace **Bus** 3, 157, 249, 410, 432, 450, 468
The house is not wheelchair accessible

The rooms in this grand Victorian house have been beautifully decorated by Sue
Haigh, the textile-designer owner, whose lovely quilts cover the beds. Coming down
to breakfast is like sitting down to a banquet, with homemade jam, marmalade, baked
goods and many different kinds of tea on the table. Sue is also happy to cook dinner
for guests and she can accommodate vegan, gluten-free, diabetic and other special
diets. When it is sunny, sit in the pretty garden at the rear surrounded by rosemary,
peonies and a Japanese maple which turns bright red in autumn. A lone grey heron
often visits, curious about the fish in the small pond. If you listen carefully, owls can
be heard hooting at night in this tranquil street.

TheWesley

81–103 Euston Street, NW1 2EZ ☎ 020 7380 0001
www.thewesley.co.uk
Tube Euston, Warren Street **Bus** 30, 59, 73, 205
TheWesley is wheelchair accessible

TheWesley is a welcoming, independent, 4-star ethical hotel with 100 rooms, located in a handsome Art Deco building close to Euston Station. The bedrooms are simply furnished in muted grey and cream, creating a calm, quiet atmosphere. There is a feel-good factor staying here – you will find locally sourced food on the breakfast menu and, as the hotel is a social enterprise, all profits go to an educational charity. The restaurant menu is not ascetic, however, and you can order a Fuller's Honeydew ale, a glass of wine or just a gingerbeer. With 18 single rooms, this is also a very safe place to stay if you are travelling alone.

The Alma Hotel
499 Old York Road, Wandsworth SW18 1TF ☎ 020 8870 2537
www.almawandsworth.com
Train Wandsworth Town **Bus** 28, 37, 44, 87, 156, 170, 219, 270, 295, 337, C3
There is one ground-floor accessible room

The Alma has some of the most stylish rooms in London. Each one is different, and
the striking wallpapers and luxurious velvet-covered armchairs make this feel like
a rather special place to stay. The restaurant and bar beneath the boutique hotel
both play music, but you can ask for dinner – dishes such as pan-fried monkfish with
clams and lemon risotto – to be brought to your quiet room. If you don't want to get up
in the morning, you can also order breakfast in bed and enjoy croissants and toast in
peace and quiet. The hotel was refurbished in recent years so looks very fashionable,
and is one of the best-kept secrets in South-West London.

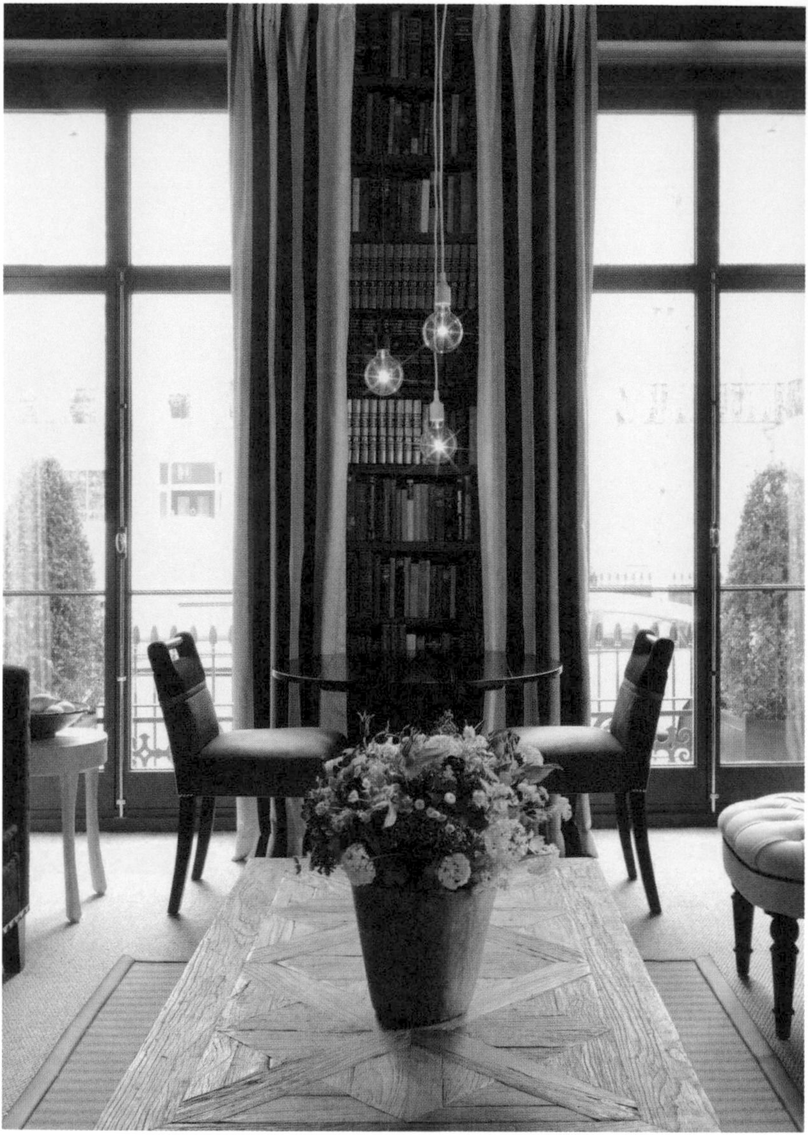

Number Sixteen

16 Sumner Place, South Kensington SW7 3EG ☎ 020 7589 5232
www.firmdalehotels.com/london/number-sixteen
Tube South Kensington **Bus** 14, 49, 70, 74, 345, 360, 414, 430
The hotel is wheelchair accessible

Number Sixteen is a beautiful luxury hotel not far from the Victoria & Albert and
Natural History Museums. It has beautiful *objets d'art* on display, brought back by the
discerning owner, Kit Kemp, from her travels around the world. The interior design
is visually stunning – from the black-and-white chequered mirror and mustard-
and-lavender curtains in the library to the hand-stitched white quilts on the beds.
Whether you prefer to sit in the exquisite garden at the rear or have breakfast in the
conservatory, this is a very restful place. You can even book a massage, aromatherapy
or anti-oxidant skin treatment in the privacy of your own room with their partner
organisation, Soholistic.

Index